and kindness for weakness, because she is the strongest, most diplomatic no-bs woman I have come across. I will always be indebted to Fabiana because she made me push past my insecurities and realize my full potential.

–Tatiyana Akers

Fabiana is highly intuitive, has strong emotional intelligence, is passionate, and has high integrity. She will do as she says she will. It will always happen because she will always do what's right.

–Clinton Allen

Fabiana is an endless inspiration to me and so many who know her because she is grounded in truth, honesty, and purpose, which she exemplifies as a leader and mentor. She shines with intellect, humor, grace, and an unmatched savviness at navigating and surmounting any challenge.

–Liz Archibald

Fabiana is a force of nature. Her no-nonsense approach to leadership demonstrates true grit, resilience, and competence. When we met, we instantly connected professionally and personally. We share a high level of intuitiveness, courage, and passion to help others and build successful, top-performing teams. Fabiana is a source of calm in a storm combined with intuition, integrity, and focused action to make her truly crisis capable. Her book is a must read for all!

–Garrett Ingram, CEO at Cipla Therapeutics, Inc.

CRISIS CAPABLE

FABIANA LACERCA-ALLEN

CRISIS
CAPABLE

BUILDING YOUR CAPACITY
TO SURVIVE AND SUCCEED
IN EVERY ENVIRONMENT

Advantage | Books

Published by Advantage Books, Charleston, South Carolina.
An imprint of Advantage Media.

ADVANTAGE is a registered trademark, and the Advantage colophon is a trademark of Advantage Media Group, Inc.

Printed in the United States of America.

10 9 8 7 6 5 4 3 2 1

ISBN: 979-8-89188-011-5 (Hardcover)
ISBN: 979-8-89188-012-2 (eBook)

Library of Congress Control Number: 2024914340

Cover design by Lance Buckley.
Layout design by Matthew Morse.

This publication is designed to provide accurate and authoritative information in regard to the subject matter covered. It is sold with the understanding that the publisher is not engaged in rendering legal, accounting, or other professional services. If legal advice or other expert assistance is required, the services of a competent professional person should be sought.

Advantage Books is an imprint of Advantage Media Group. Advantage Media helps busy entrepreneurs, CEOs, and leaders write and publish a book to grow their business and become the authority in their field. Advantage authors comprise an exclusive community of industry professionals, idea-makers, and thought leaders. For more information go to **advantagemedia.com**.

To the warriors in my life, and to those who are working to be warriors in their own way.

CONTENTS

INTRODUCTION 1

1. RED SHADOWS 9
2. THE MATH TUTOR 17
3. SIX MONTHS 31
4. THE RELOCATION 53
5. EVERY SIGN TELLS A STORY 69
6. THE DIFFERENT SHADES OF GRAY 87
7. FINDING A NEW PATH 97
8. SELECTING YOUR TRIBE 111
9. SPEAKING YOUR MIND IN LEADERSHIP 131

CONCLUSION 141

ACKNOWLEDGMENTS 145

ABOUT THE AUTHOR 147

INTRODUCTION

When I was growing up, the living room in our home held a specific purpose. My father would always use it to have important conversations. If someone distinguished or in his network came to our house—as they often did—they would head to the living room together.

During those times, everyone else in the house, including my sister and me, knew that no one else should join them for specific discussions. My father, who was a businessman and leading figure in Argentina at the time, wanted some discussions to be privately held because they had to do with the country's well-being: democracy and overthrowing the military dictatorship were at stake. Still, I can vividly recall the strong curiosity I had to listen in as a six-year-old. I wanted to know what was going on because I wanted to make a difference too. Even as a young child, I wanted to be involved in making things better for my country and family.

It was an intense era in many ways. One time, I heard one of my father's friends say he was being followed. My father told him to lie low and that he would try to see what was going on. That was the conversation I heard—the fear in his voice, my father trying to reassure him. Days later, he was shot and killed. When I learned the news, I went to tell my father that I had heard their discussion. I felt bad, and it weighed

1

on me that I had heard something I shouldn't have heard. He told me, "You should listen to information when you're ready to do something with it." He didn't want me listening to his conversations because he felt I was too young to do anything about them. When you know something, you have a responsibility. It's up to you to decide what you will do with the information you have. The lesson learned was that you should participate in conversations where you can make a difference. Information is power as long as you can do something with it.

Perhaps that's because, even back then, I had a strong inclination to be aware of my surroundings. In fact, being observant and mindful of what was happening at any given moment was a critical part of our daily lives. My family was living in Argentina during the 1970s, a period of unrest. When I was young, the military had power, and there were other groups fighting for control. Terrorist organizations threatened and kidnapped many during this time too. Some citizens faced a fate of "desaparecidos" (disappeared), as they were kidnapped and never seen again.[1] These events had such a rippling impact on everyone. Even if you weren't directly kidnaped, you were affected by what was going on. There was really no escaping in that sense.

My father held democratic values, and his views didn't align with the military's rule. However, he had strong ties in upper political and business circles, given his education and family ties. He had attended the military academy in his youth, per the custom of well-to-do families that wanted disciplined training for their children. He was absolutely brilliant and notably the top student during his time there—but he greatly opposed the military and forceful actions. His principles wouldn't allow for violence. Though he was a natural leader,

---

1   "Argentina Background," 2001, Human Rights Watch, https://www.hrw.org/reports/2001/argentina/argen1201-02.htm.

his style emulated an appearance of calm and control. When he spoke, others listened.

What he said during some of those countless conversations in our living room, I will never know. I did, however, perceive that he played an important role in many decisions. He was instrumental in restoring democracy in Argentina and served on the first cabinet after it was reestablished. With his stance and position in society came risks. Our family was among the initial targets of the terrorist organizations. Later, we were threatened by the military junta that wanted to remain in power, and that meant danger.

Though I was young, I innately knew that horrible things could and did happen. I had heard of and knew others who had been killed, kidnapped, or "desaparecidos," and I didn't want any of my loved ones to be among that group.

I also didn't want my father to become a victim or a casualty based on his principles. The four of us—my father, mother, sister, and myself—lived constantly alert and ready to act as needed. We relied on guards, watchdogs, and technology to be protected. Still, we learned early on that the best protection was knowing who was around you, who you could trust, and what was the optimal way to move around in the country based on the situation at the time. One wrong move and our entire world could change. This reality was interwoven into our daily lives.

And so, as I drifted off to sleep during those early years, the occurrences of my daytime events would seep into my dreams—or rather, nightmares. In one I particularly recall, my dream began with my father in the basket of a hot-air balloon. The vessel was on the ground, and I stood nearby. Then, the hot-air balloon lifted, and my father drifted up, slowly climbing into the sky. Higher and higher he floated, flying away from me.

Still on the ground, I watched him drift further away from me. I held out my arms in an attempt to pull him back to the ground, but I couldn't reach him. No matter what I tried, I could not bring him back. I thought to myself, "He's gone from my life."

I woke up crying. Tears poured from my eyes as I bolted out of bed and went to look for my father. I found him in the living room and realized it was only a nightmare.

He was sitting alone on the sofa. No other important guests were there at the time. I ran to him, still sobbing, and pleaded, "I don't want you to die! I don't want you to die! And I don't want to die either!"

I went on to tell him the details of my dream. Sitting next to him that night, I shared the awful image of him floating away from me in a hot-air balloon, outside of my grasp forever and disappearing from my life.

When I had finished my tale of sorrow, my father didn't scold me for being out of bed. He didn't send me back immediately either. He looked at me very seriously.

Then, he said, in his calm, assuring voice, "Oh…we're all going to die. So don't worry about it."

He continued, "We are like flowers. We grow, we blossom, and we die. We're all going to die, so don't worry about it. Worry about what you're going to live for. *Some things are worth dying for. For everything else, you need a plan.*"

Those very words started me on my professional path, and these are things I live by for today.

With his soothing, practical words, my tears slowed and eventually came to a stop. His announcement of the reality of our situation, dire as it was in some ways, helped me to find a new perspective. He had emphasized, in a delicate manner, the value of living with a purpose. Those words stuck with me that night, and during the next days and years. Now, as I lead and guide others, they continue to be a driving force.

His encouragement to have a plan remained, too. That night, I sat on the sofa next to my father in the room of important conversations hearing about the need to be prepared. He was living amid a political, economic, and social crisis during that time, and he knew the difference that having a plan could make. When danger arose, if you were aware of what was going on and knew what to do, your life could be saved.

THE DIFFERENCE HAVING A PLAN CAN MAKE

In a way, recovering from my childhood nightmare based on the fear of losing my loved ones was my very first crisis management plan. I found myself returning to those words time and again during the days and years that followed. Some things were worth dying for. For everything else, plan.

And I did. My first plan was pretty good for a six-year-old. I told my parents that if I ever was kidnapped, I would ask the kidnappers to buy me dulce de leche. That way, my parents would know where to find me—I would be at a place where a lot of dulce de leche was sold. I happened to like the treat too. For me, this plan created a win-win.

All joking aside, as I moved to the United States later in life for college and stayed to pursue a career in corporate America, I carried that theme of having a plan with me. The principle I learned that night, along with the other core values I gathered from my father, family, and life experiences of my youth, opened the doors to opportunities.

When I was a young professional, I rose in ranks quickly and earned my credentials fast. My superiors recognized that with my upbringing and attitude, I had emotional intelligence, self-confidence, and an ability to think clearly and strategically in complicated and tense situations. I had navigated crises even as a youth and managed through them. I was a warrior, and I knew how to inspire and teach others to be warriors, too.

Today, I'm a C-level compliance executive with more than thirty years of experience and have held senior roles at some of the world's most widely recognized companies. Throughout the years, I have successfully advised and influenced top leaders on critical matters such as product commercialization and marketing, FDA and OIG compliance, mergers and acquisitions, joint ventures, and corporate governance. I've become an expert at building strategic compliance programs across Fortune 100 organizations and have successfully negotiated and implemented corporate integrity agreements and deferred prosecution agreements for US corporations with extensive global operations.

As I reflect on my career and personal life, I'm convinced that having a reason to live and creating a plan can help anyone build strategies for both their professional and personal paths. The right skills and the commitment to your set of values play an essential role in navigating a crisis. Just as I have drawn on my unique background and traits, you can use your own experiences to bring a powerful and diverse voice to the table. As you move into leadership roles, you'll be able to build your own team of warriors—that is, staff members who can be trained and equipped to be able to respond rapidly and effectively during a critical moment.

In the pages that follow, I'll walk you through the chapters of my own life, with the goal of providing lessons I've learned along the way that can be applied in both the corporate and personal realms. We'll begin by delving into a time when my family was in imminent danger, and I learned, firsthand, the power of intuition and situational awareness. We'll move on to a critical moment when I faced kidnapping attempts and leaned into my ability to quickly observe and assess a situation to make a decision. I'll tell of a time my father taught me the "Six-Month Rule"—meaning you shouldn't make decisions that you don't have to make, and by waiting until you have better information you can gain clarity on what to do. I'll share how this can be applied to corporate America and leadership roles. If you have patience, adaptability, and can think critically, you'll set yourself apart from others who do not. You'll be able to look below the surface to find out what's really going on, identify challenges, and then create solutions.

As we move on, I'll tell of a time when I negotiated for a relocation package and realized that another worker at the company asked for a relocation package as well—for ten times more than what I requested. We both received what we asked for, and I committed to always self-assess and advocate for myself from that point on. You'll learn the power of knowing your worth and then understanding how to negotiate to get the results you want.

I'll also discuss the importance of being socially aware and picking up signs, and how these skills can be applied to all aspects of our lives. If you have the opportunity to help someone else move up or improve their current situation, it will likely be incredibly fulfilling for you, and they will also be motivated to reach out and lend a hand to others they know.

We'll study how the negotiating process can play out and recognize that we all react to risk differently and process information in many ways. While there are no clear "black-and-white" settings, I've learned to embrace the "grays," to interpret the factors at play, and to make sense of the nuances—and I'll show you how to do the same.

Have you ever walked away from a situation that didn't seem right? I have. I'm a firm believer in living according to your values, and I respect others who do the same. We'll spend some time exploring how to let your values guide you and leverage them to make key decisions. Along those same lines, we'll look at how to surround yourself with individuals who have different capabilities but the same values. When this is done the right way, you'll add incredible layers of expertise, knowledge, and emotional intelligence to your team.

Let's face it. The world is changing fast, and to keep up and move ahead, it's essential to know how to make quick decisions, maneuver through tricky settings, and apply emotional intelligence to every situation. When you do, you'll notice a difference in both yourself and your surroundings. Get ready to uplevel your life, to ask for what you're worth, and best of all, to get it. And when you do, you can look to the next person who may not be able to speak for themselves and reach out a hand to help them step up too.

Together we can inspire change, build diversity, and be prepared for whatever comes next. In the pages that follow, I'll lay out the tools you need to lead confidently in a crisis and successfully navigate crucial situations. Because at the end of the day, a life guided by values is one worth living and fighting for.

CHAPTER 1

RED SHADOWS

"They're too close," Valeria, my sister, told my parents and me. "They're looking at us."

She was just four years old when she spoke those words while we were at our weekend home on the river in rural Argentina. She could see that something was out of pattern. Usually, we saw lights from the guards that were watching us, as they made their rounds. They always walked the same path, so their beams came in at a similar angle. This time, however, she noticed that the lights seemed closer than usual.

We had arrived at the weekend home to get away from our city residence for a couple of days, as we often did. This time, my sister realized a change in the pattern. Someone besides the guards, she was convinced, was watching us through the home's large bay windows.

Indeed, we were being watched, my parents assured her. They assumed it was the security guards who patrolled the perimeter of the property night and day. It was the 1970s in Argentina, during a time that the military dictatorship was in power. The group went after those who threatened their rule, and those who did not share their thinking or values. There were also revolutionary groups opposing the military regime. One of these was a terrorist group called the Ejército Revolucionario del Pueblo. Most people were caught in the middle, and it was hard to know with whom to align or choose. Though my father didn't subscribe to harmful acts, he was a leading figure and businessman during that time, and he held influence in many circles. His views, which differed from the military, put him and our family at risk.

Being surrounded with security guards was part of daily life for my younger sister and myself. While we had to be constantly monitored and were continually aware of the danger at hand, we carried on. Even as children, we knew not to tell people where we were going to be and when we would arrive. For his part, my father maintained his belief that democracy should prevail, and he wasn't in agreement with the violent acts and oppression he saw around him during that time in history in Argentina. During this time, with so much disruption and fighting for power that the people in Argentina suffered, human rights were violated, and everyone knew. It was hard to live a regular life amid so many kidnappings and disappearances.

So when my sister noticed that something seemed off and recognized that the pattern had been broken, she said something. She felt that whoever was looking into the window was closer than the distance that the security guards usually kept while walking the perimeter of the property. As such a young kid, it was hard for the adults to believe her. They simply shrugged off her observations and assured both of us that all was fine.

But it wasn't. And I knew it. I believed my sister. I, too, sensed that something was wrong. At a very young age, we had learned to trust and rely on each other. The hours that followed brought defining moments in our lives and ultimately equipped me with greater self-confidence and a stronger reliance on my intuition.

* * *

Before I continue my story, I want you to consider a few questions. Firstly, what do you do when a situation doesn't seem right? More importantly, how do you know if something is amiss? What are the signs to look for? And what skills do you need to have to quickly assess a scene and make a decision?

The following sections will address all these questions. I'll share what happened after my sister thought she saw someone watching us too closely. I'll expand on how we both intuitively doubted that the figures in the window were really the security guards, an important concern at a time when kidnappings and disappearances took place so often that we didn't have the luxury of "comfort," or feeling 100 percent safe, at any time. I'll also share insights on how to have situational awareness and ways to recognize and rely on your intuition. When you're able to harness these capabilities, the impact that you'll see in both business and personal settings can be significant and lasting.

A DREAM BASED ON INTUITION

After my sister stated that she thought we were being watched by someone besides the guards and my parents dismissed her thoughts, our concerns continued. In addition to the large bay windows where something seemed off, the home had other entry points. The side door coming from the pool was particularly noticeable. It was paneled with red glass. If someone stood on the outside of the side door, you could see their shadow from inside.

That night, after my sister saw something out of pattern at the bay window, I had a dream. In it, I saw red shadows on the other side of the red glass moving toward the house. The image shook me awake and out of the dream. I ran to my parents' room and woke them up. I told them of the dream and how I had seen something shifting outside the red glass-paneled door. I described the shadows that were so frightening.

Just as they had told my sister that nothing was out of the ordinary, they did the same with me. They calmly explained to me that we were safe and sent me back to bed. I went, although I wasn't convinced that all was okay.

MINUTES TO SPARE

When we spent the weekends at our home on the river, we usually returned to the city on Monday. Our typical routine was to leave the weekend house at 6:00 a.m. on the start of the work and school day. My sister and I would be dressed in our uniforms, ready to be taken straight to school. That weekend, despite my sister's observance and my bad dream, we continued with the schedule and aimed to leave around 6:00 a.m. to get to school on time.

However, at 5:00 a.m. that Monday, the phone rang. My father answered it and spoke to the other person on the line. When he hung up, he decided we would leave early. By then, the family was up, and we followed my father's instructions.

We packed during the next few minutes and bid farewell to the staff who maintained the weekend home. We rolled away from the weekend home before our usual departure time of 6:00 a.m., headed back to our main residence and then on to a day of school.

About fifteen minutes after we left the weekend home, sixteen heavily armed men burst into it. They wore masks and carried guns.

They wanted to harm us. They searched the home for my father, my mother, my sister, and myself…and didn't find any of us.

The staff who maintained the house and property were still on-site, and the heavily armed men found them. They were part of the Ejército Revolucionario del Pueblo. The heavily armed men threatened the people who worked for us. They fired off their guns, and some employees were hurt. The group destroyed everything inside the house and painted on the walls.

That terrorist group had been watching us, just as my sister noticed. While the security guards did walk around our property, they always stayed a certain distance from the windows. The terrorists, for their part, wanted to get a close view of us as they prepared to storm the home and harm us. They had gone up close to the bay window to see inside and check on us. That was why my sister sensed something was out of pattern. Indeed, the lights had been closer than the beams from the regular guards.

I thought back to my dream. Did I see something like my sister? Or did I instinctively sense that something was off? Regardless, the dream I had served as a warning of what was to come. Had our family not left the weekend home early, the story of that evening and following morning would have had a different ending.

THE NEED FOR SITUATIONAL AWARENESS

I never forgot that trip to our weekend home. While we were fortunate to have left in time, I learned a critical lesson from the event. I recognized the impact that being able to notice the surroundings could have. I placed a high value on leaning into my intuition, as it could sense if something was amiss. By trusting it, I could react in a way that had a greater chance of a positive outcome.

Later in life, when I was grown and had three kids of my own, I would often take them out and test their situational awareness. We might walk through a crowd, and I would ask them to quickly describe an individual. I taught them how to absorb the details in a room and notice signs of something being astray. A person with a winter coat on during summer, for example, could be a red flag. It would be considered something outside of a pattern. Or spotting an individual whom you have already seen twice before during that week could be a sign of danger. Why are you seeing them for the third time?

Even today, just as I did during my early years, I find it highly important to rapidly absorb a setting and notice anything out of place. In all areas, it could make a big difference. It could mean success over failure, escape over capture, or life over death. In the case of a crisis, if you're aware of the situation, you can make decisions faster. You may be able to gain an advantage by being one step ahead of those who are distracted or unfocused.

LEADING THROUGH CHANGE

Supposed you notice something is amiss in a tense situation that is rapidly changing. What do you do next? What if you don't have all the information at hand? Should you take the time to find out all the details?

The most amazing leaders I have come across are the ones who can assess a situation and make the right decision while staying levelheaded. Often if you freeze and don't move, you increase your risk. Thus, moving is critical, and by being aware of the surroundings, leaders are better equipped to take action.

While my family escaped the terrorist attack at our weekend home by leaving early, there would be other tough times ahead. My sister and I would need to continue to rely on our intuitive natures and constantly be aware of what was going on around us. These skills would help us navigate the threats and respond in a clear, instinctive way.

As you consider your own life and career, I encourage you to think about patterns. If you haven't paid attention to your surroundings in the past, start today. Look for details, such as what people are wearing and how they are interacting with others. Check for changes and take note when something falls out of place.

Also keep in mind the importance of planning, along with being ready to adapt as needed. During investigations in legal matters, for instance, you need to know what the next steps are. You might list out who to interview and lay out an initial strategy to follow. Then, as new information becomes available, be ready to make adjustments and change. Listen to your intuition as you navigate an investigation and stay calm so you can readily assess the situation. You might listen to someone being interviewed and sense that the facts don't add up. After further research, you could discover that the person's story doesn't match the evidence. You can then make a decision based on this new information.

Whenever you sense something is off, lean into what your senses are telling you. If the situation is at work, it could mean speaking up and sharing your concern with others. If it occurs in your personal life, it could be a sign that you should leave the setting or get help. By recognizing and valuing your intuition, you'll be well prepared to face both the minor and critical moments and make the right decisions for yourself and others on your team.

KEY TAKEAWAYS

- Act decisively. In rapidly changing and tense situations, freezing can increase risk. Leaders need to be able to assess a situation and move toward action.

- Be aware of your surroundings. Stay vigilant and rely on your intuition to navigate threats and respond.

- Pay attention to patterns. Notice details and monitor people's behaviors and interactions.

- Go with your intuition. It will help you recognize when something is missing or off.

CHAPTER 2

THE MATH TUTOR

Have you ever found yourself trying to escape from somewhere? Have you ever been in a circumstance that you wanted to leave? Perhaps you have had a time when a plan for an escape wasn't specifically stated, but you had a sense that it was time to get out and get out fast.

That's exactly what we'll be discussing in this chapter. I'll share a story about getting tutored in math and how it impacted my security risk at the time. I'll include the choices I made and explain why I acted as I did.

Then, we'll spend some time evaluating how you can do the same, and how you can build emotional intelligence. This skill, which is often touted as important but may not be as readily taught as multiplication and division in school systems, can help you do more than pass your tests. It could save your life, put you in a position of leadership, or help you decide who to choose to be in a position of authority. In your personal life, knowing how to navigate critical situations and understanding ways to avoid risk can enable you to develop healthy, productive relationships with others who support you and your goals.

When I was about fourteen years old, I flunked math while attending school in Argentina. My father soon learned of the news, and he approached me to talk about it. As I've mentioned, he had always emphasized the importance of planning for everything. So, when the topic about my poor math grade came up between us, he asked me, "What's your plan?"

At the time, I didn't have a great strategy outlined. The discussion between us over my math scores turned to one of my father's other key teachings, which was, "If you don't have a plan, someone else will have a plan for you, and you might not like it." To deal with my flunking math, he set up an arrangement to help me catch up on my studies. And, as he predicted, I wasn't thrilled by it.

My father's plan involved me being tutored by his former math teacher. I was taken aback by the news. To me, as a teenager, my father's old math teacher seemed ancient. She was probably seventy or eighty years old by then (I never learned her exact age). My father contacted her and set up a cadence in which I would go to her residence twice a week after school. There I would study math with her for an hour to help me raise my math grade. It was important to my father to choose a reliable, trustworthy source, given the instability the country faced at the time.

The sessions began, and a new routine developed. Since I had to go twice a week to the tutor's home to study math, we set up a schedule which involved a driver taking me to her place and picking me up. Occasionally, my father would drop me off and come to get me. If he did, it was always arranged well ahead of time. We had to keep procedures clear for security purposes.

Given this, my new situation created a change in schedule. Moreover, it proposed a risk we would have to deal with. Getting dropped off and picked up from the same point, during the same days every week and at the same times, meant that others could track my route. They might find me in the "X," which refers the point where an attack could happen.

SAYING "NO" TO THE BELL

After school, I would be driven to the home of my father's former math teacher on Tuesdays and Thursdays. I would arrive at 5:00 p.m. and leave at 6:00 p.m. The tutor lived on the top floor of a tall apartment building, and to get inside her place, I would first enter the lobby. There I would ring the buzzer for her apartment. Through the intercom system, I would speak to the math tutor and identify myself. She would then press a button to open a door which led to her floor and home. The driver waited while I did this and would only leave after I had safely entered to go to the tutor's apartment.

Then, I would stay at her flat until 6:00 p.m. At that time, I would get picked up, and whoever was getting me—my father or a driver—would ring the bell in the lobby when they arrived. They would then speak into the intercom system and identify themselves to the teacher, who would listen from inside the safety of her apartment. I knew that I should be ready for the 6:00 p.m. ring of the bell, as it signaled the end of my session.

My father, meticulous about planning, kept the procedures well outlined. Everything had to be arranged with care, including the scheduled math sessions, who would be taking me, and who would pick me up. It was important to communicate in detail with everyone involved, because that way we would all know what to expect and could be prepared.

One day, I was dropped off at the usual 5:00 p.m. by one of our family's drivers. Getting inside the math teacher's place was simple and straightforward. I arrived on time, rang the bell, and was let inside, and the tutoring session began. I planned on staying until 6:00 p.m., when the lesson would end, and I would be escorted home. Under that premise, the teacher and I began the session.

That day, however, the bell rang at 5:45 p.m., fifteen minutes ahead of schedule. The sound resonated for an unusually long time. It was a loud ring, as if someone was pressing hard on the buzzer. As the noise moved the apartment, it caught the attention of both my math tutor and me. The teacher got up and went to speak into the intercom. When she came back, she said, "It's your father. He's outside, waiting for you. He's here to pick you up. It's time for you to go home."

I remained sitting. Looking at my father's former math teacher, I replied, "It's not my father."

Returning my gaze, she said, "Well, I've known that man for longer than you have. Who are you to tell me it's not your father?"

Still, I didn't shift. Instead, I explained that whoever she had spoken to, I was sure it wasn't my father. I explained my reasoning too. "First, he would never ring the bell that way. The sound was a long beep, which is much longer than my father would ring." I knew that my father, a well-educated and respectful man, would consider it polite to ring quickly. Holding the bell for an extended period and ringing loudly were not actions I had ever seen or heard him do. I added that the driver was supposed to come for me up that day and not anyone else.

"Most importantly," I continued, "my father would never, ever pick me up early from a class." Again, I knew how he would think and act. I was aware that my father was the type to adhere to schedules. Even if something atrocious had happened, he would reason that picking me up early wouldn't make a difference in the bigger scheme of things. He would want me to finish and to do what had to be done first. Then, he would pick me up at the set hour and deal with whatever matter was at hand. To him, picking me up fifteen minutes early from an important math session would not be an option.

In the end, I refused to go at 5:45 p.m. I insisted on waiting until 6:00 p.m., which was the time the session was scheduled to finish. When the clock turned to the hour, my math teacher and I looked out the window. On the street below, we could see the driver pull up—just as he always did. Then, he entered the lobby and rang the bell, exactly as planned. As it turned out, it had not been my father who had arrived early and tried to take me out of class fifteen minutes early.

THE VALUE OF EMOTIONAL INTELLIGENCE

That day, when someone else tried to pick me up from the tutoring session, if I had not relied on my senses and previous knowledge, the outcome could have been very different. A certain feeling, or intuition, can be hard to quantify. It's not the same as writing out a multiplication table or memorizing a series of math facts. Still, it is a skill that is so important. If you have a high IQ and can carry out advanced technical tasks, but have a minimum sense of awareness, you could have a lower chance of surviving a crisis.

WHAT IS EMOTIONAL INTELLIGENCE?

The phrase "emotional intelligence" is not necessarily a new trend. The term was introduced initially in 1990 by researchers John Mayer and Peter Salovey.[2] It was later popularized by Daniel Goleman, a psy-

---

2   Lauren Landry, "Why Emotional Intelligence Is Important in Leadership," Harvard Business School Online, April 3, 2019, https://online.hbs.edu/blog/post/emotional-intelligence-in-leadership.

chologist who highlighted the importance of emotional intelligence in leadership. He listed five elements associated with this trait, which are self-awareness, self-regulation, motivation, empathy, and social skills.[3] Goleman told *Harvard Business Review*, "The most effective leaders are alike in one crucial way: They all have a high degree of what has come to be known as emotional intelligence. It's not that IQ and technical skills are irrelevant. They do matter, but ... they are entry-level requirements for executive positions."

When I think of emotional intelligence, I consider it to be the ability to recognize your strengths and weaknesses. It's also the capability of understanding how other people react to you. Emotional intelligence involves taking this information and knowing how you can use it to communicate with others and work together. It includes the capacity to observe a situation before you have all the information before you. It encases listening to your intuition and having the courage to act.

EMOTIONAL INTELLIGENCE IN DECISION-MAKING

Amazing leaders tend to share certain characteristics, including emotional intelligence. I am often drawn to those in authority who are comfortable enough in their skin to take the information they have at hand and use it to make a choice. They're aware that they'll have to live with the consequences of their actions, and they're okay with that.

The reality is that you often won't have all the data that you would ideally like to see before deciding on a matter. Due to time constraints and the risks involved, you might not be able to wait until you have

---

3   Kendra Cherry, "5 Key Emotional Intelligence Skills," Verywell Mind, December 31, 2023, https://www.verywellmind.com/components-of-emotional-intelligence-2795438.

every detail. You'll need to set a direction for others to follow and then take action to move forward.

I always encourage others to lean into their prior knowledge and listen to what their intuition tells them. If you do this, you might find a solution that makes sense to you. What you decide to do may not be the most well-liked, widely accepted path. And it might not be what most people would do. In my case, at the math tutoring session, I had to explain my position and reasoning to someone who was my senior. It was the right thing to do, but it wasn't necessarily easy. For me, it was worthwhile to stick with my decision. My math tutor eventually realized this too, particularly when she saw the driver arrive at 6:00 p.m., right on schedule.

When navigating a critical situation, if you can stay calm and converse openly, you may be able to explain your motives and gain the support of others. By drawing on emotional intelligence, you'll also be able to accept what happens after you make a decision.

I recall visiting my child Nico's school when she was younger and watching her on the playground. She stood off to the side and observed the other kids playing. The principal at the school assured me her approach was a wise one. "She's seeing what's happening, and then she'll make a choice regarding when and with whom she wants to interact," he explained. Nico knew already at an early age that it's important to pay attention to what's going on around her. It takes courage to make the right choices and to influence your surroundings accordingly. It will help you develop a strategy and choose your friends carefully.

Leveling the Playing Field

One of the advantages of using situational awareness to navigate a setting is that it can direct your mind to new possibilities. For me, at the math tutoring session, thinking of all the possible actions I could take led to my staying rather than accepting the call to leave. In work, this may mean coming up with an idea that no one else has yet considered. If you're open to thinking outside the box, you could present options that are creative—and that get results.

When I was a junior lawyer, I spent some time representing a powerful American company. The organization had a partner in a different country. For several reasons, during my time with the American company, it was necessary to break ties with the foreign corporation. When we moved forward to carry this out, it was opposed by the foreign partner. The foreign partner responded by suing the American corporation. Moreover, the executives from the foreign branch presented the litigation in their home country. They had significant influence there, and I sensed that the judges in their own country would lean toward a decision in their favor.

After observing the string of events and thinking them over, I told my boss in the United States, "We would never win this on their ground and terms. The only way we can carry through with this is to put pressure on them in the US." I felt strongly that if we went to the foreign country, the power would be on their side.

After my boss listened to my point of view, he followed my advice. The American company sued the foreign counterpart in the United States.

This move very much leveled the playing field. Immediately, those involved on the foreign side were ready to negotiate. They wanted to find a solution. So did we. We had the start of an understanding.

I stayed on the deal to carry out the negotiations. I was very young and a new lawyer, so it might not have been logical to have me stay on such a sensitive case. However, a higher-up saw that I was able to think outside the box. Those in leadership at the company realized that my ideas led to different results. Rather than having the US executives travel to the other country, where they would not have had influence or as much power, we were able to coordinate a set of events that brought the case to the American side. And I was behind that chain of consequences.

When I suggested the idea, I didn't have all of the information in my hands. I didn't know for sure what the result would be. However, I knew enough to be confident that the playing field could be leveled if the case came to the US side. After all, we were working for an American company.

In the end, we gave the American company a new chance to settle the matter on a level playing field. We gained an advantage for them, and it was due to a focus on the art of the issue. Rather than arguing facts, I shifted the location of the negotiations to a place where I knew the American company could have a greater chance of success. I used emotional intelligence to think through where the other side was coming from, what mattered to them, and how the American company could work with them to come to a reasonable solution.

Making the Deal

Another time early in my career, I traveled to a country in Latin America with another lawyer who was about ten years my senior. We went there on behalf of an international company to negotiate a deal. Even though my coworker was older than me, I immediately sensed that his knowledge of the country was limited. When we arrived, we were escorted in armored vehicles to our destination, which was common practice for that area and period in history. I had frequently traveled in well-protected vehicles in my youth and was familiar with the norms of the region. My coworker, on the other hand, asked to be the driver. He wanted to play music, too. I calmly explained that there would be no music playing, because the drivers had to pay attention and listen to what was going on around them.

The negotiations with the Latin American firm were set to take place the following day. We had agreed, internally, ahead of time that there was a clause we could not agree to. If we did, it would break the deal. With those limits in place, we entered the room to begin the discussion.

Seated on my side, the senior lawyer began in a very direct way. The tactics used were quite aggressive and didn't go far with the Latin American recipients. These executives were extremely socially adept and well prepared. I could tell as I watched them that they were not likely to respond with a proposed agreement when presented with such hostile arguments.

I was right, and the discussion dragged along without a resolution. Finally, my coworker called for a break and left the room. He stated that we all needed some time and then we would resume.

I stayed, and so did the executives from the other side. I then calmly began my own discussion. I explained, in a steady and respectful tone, that there was a clause we could not give in to. I showed them which one it was and added that I was sure, if they were in my position, they would have the same approach.

After hearing my point of view, and seeing that they were being treated well, the executives started to find points on which we could agree. We were able to work up a deal that we could all be comfortable with. And, thanks to emotional intelligence, rather than straight-up disagreements, we resolved the situation.

As you consider your own negotiations at work and at home, keep in mind that we all want to feel that we are winning. Everyone has a desire to be respected and to be heard. If you can make the other party see that you are listening to them, they may be more receptive to your own opinion. If you can carry out these conversations strategically, you'll go far. Once people feel they are treated with respect, you can often move into the next steps of negotiating and come to an agreement that works for everyone.

GETTING OUT OF THE X

In conversations about security, you might hear phrases about the "X." Getting out of the X refers to moving away from the place where somebody else can hurt you. Think about this: If someone is planning to harm you, they need to know how to find you. They might investigate your home address and then monitor how often you leave your place. They could watch to see the hour you typically go to work and the time you return. Or they might search for other places you go to on a regular basis. If you always park in a certain spot when you get groceries, and shop at the same time over the weekend, they might stake out a place on your route where they could attack you. It could be in the parking lot at the time you usually shop. You'll need to get out of this spot to avoid getting hurt.

When I developed the strategy to file a lawsuit in the United States against the foreign branch, we determined where the executives from the other country would be landing on American soil. With this knowledge, we established a spot where they could be arrested. Similarly, in certain instances you face, you may want to determine an outcome, which could be the best location to find the other party. This can be helpful if you need to locate someone or are trying to bring someone over to your area of influence.

Moving to the other side, you'll usually want to avoid situations where you could be a target. For instance, if there is an X where someone could find and hurt you, you'll want to take a different route if possible. Learning to get out of the X is a skill that can be taught.

When I became a parent and had younger children, I trained them to absorb details about the environment quickly. I might tell them to look at someone in a crowd or behind us and then describe them. We would talk about how tall the person was, the color of their clothing, and any other physical attributes we noticed. I might say, "That person is 270 pounds, 6'5", and has dark hair." Being able to quickly identify individuals and your surroundings can give you information that might be useful. Your brain will learn to process information quickly.

We have carried out exercises to help raise awareness about an individual's surroundings. We might send team members out to shop at five stores. Before they begin their venture, we inform them that they will be followed in some of the shops. For instance, a staff member might be told that someone will be watching them in three of the five places. They then have to walk through the stores and browse the merchandise, staying alert to their surroundings to identify who is following them. They must report back to us regarding what the person looked like. They need to know details about where and when they were followed.

When I'm speaking with others about staying safe, I often say, "Get out of the X." This means the goal is to avoid any situation that could be damaging to you in any aspect. For me, as a teenager when I was getting tutored in math, the X was the apartment building where I would get dropped off and picked up twice a week at the same time. In other life settings, it could refer to staying away from places that could harm your reputation. For instance, if you're running for a position as a politician, you may not want to be spotted in a protest (especially if the rally doesn't align with the messaging you're sharing with the media for your campaign).

Going forward, I encourage you to remember that when you work with people, you'll relate to them better if you know what motivates them. Take the time to understand their agenda and see what matters to them in real life. If you do this, you'll be surprised to find out just how many unpleasant conversations can be avoided. It all starts with knowing what to look for and how to react when you see a new situation unfold.

KEY TAKEAWAYS

- Emotional intelligence emphasizes self-awareness, empathy, and social skills to manage different situations. Effective leaders have high levels of emotional intelligence.
- When negotiating, emotional intelligence will help you see what's important to the other party, and this can help you find outcomes that benefit both parties.
- Use the information you have at hand to make decisions and be ready to accept the consequences.
- Developing situational awareness involves recognizing potential risks and opportunities in different settings.

CHAPTER 3

SIX MONTHS

In 1983, Argentina welcomed in a new government, overseen by the democratically elected President Raúl Alfonsin. This shift, in many ways, represented what my father had been dedicating his life to for the past decades. Democracy had arrived, replacing the military dictatorship which had controlled the country from 1976 until 1983.

The transition impacted households throughout Argentina. In our home, I had grown up when the country was under a different ruling power. I had learned, from a very young age, the value of doing the right thing for the right reasons, despite the surrounding dangers. I had watched my father interact with other leaders at our dinner table, as they laid out potential solutions to improve the country. I knew as I listened that they were putting their lives on the line for what they believed in.

With a democracy in place, the leaders who had advocated for the elections would now take on new roles. This included my father, who became the first state secretary of industry for the elected government. He continued to live for his values and dedicated his time to helping the country move past the years of dictatorship and into a different, improved era for its citizens.

When I think back to those years, I remember that life was good at that time. The intense life-and-death situations, laden with risk and the threat of being kidnapped, subsided. With my father's position came privileges and the chance to continue interacting with other leaders and influencers who would pave the direction for the country. It was exciting, and we could think more about social engagements and parties than before. In short, I was enjoying life!

I continued in this lifestyle, furthering my education to become a lawyer, along with my friends who were on the same path. I thought I would stay in Argentina and build my career there. After all, things were going well. I had a local boyfriend, the country was stabilizing, and I was surrounded by my family.

Imagine what happened then when my father approached me and proposed a different plan. "Whatever you want to be," he said, "you want to be the best at it. And to be the best lawyer, you need to study at the best universities." In addition to my training in Argentina, he believed that I should spend some of my educational years in the United States.

At the time, I questioned the idea. I had traveled to the United States on trips many times by then and spoke English. I had seen the country and was fluent in the language. Besides, things were so great in Argentina. Why would I leave it all?

In the end, my father convinced me that I should not make any big decisions before experiencing a situation for six months. That discussion, together with the later decisions that were made, significantly impacted the trajectory of my career and life. It wasn't always easy, but I have no regrets. It ultimately led me to a place where I felt I could make a difference and work (as my father had for so many years) to create a positive impact by living out my values.

As you absorb the following tale, take some time to think about your own life and upbringing. Perhaps there were some values that were instilled in you from early on. Maybe you faced tough decisions early in your career (or later!) that didn't seem to have a clear answer. The fact is, we will all have those critical moments in our personal and professional lives. Having a strategy to follow, such as waiting for six months before we choose a path, can provide further insight and details that will help us make the best decision. That said, there are times when you'll need to act more quickly, and we'll cover that too. When you have a mindset that is guided by long-term goals, you can even help your children and others in your life find the best path forward.

DECIDING TO BE A QUEEN—OR A LAWYER

I always knew I wanted to make a difference and have a plan. Growing up amid the strong levels of security, I watched my father do all that he could for what he believed in. He wanted a democracy for Argentina, and he used his business knowledge and political ties to work toward that goal. He preferred logic and discussion over battles and violence. That's how he fought his battle.

I also was aware that I could listen to my intuition. I could pick up on details in my environment in an instant and sense what was going on—even before it happened. I trusted what I saw and wanted to do the right thing in a way that would help others.

Shortly after the kidnapping attempt which took place at our weekend home, we returned to school. This school had played a fundamental role in my education and upbringing, and it was where I formed lifelong friends, including girls I refer to as las Margaritas.

There the teacher asked the class what they wanted to be when they were older. When it was my turn, I answered, "A queen." I was about six years old at the time.

The teacher looked at me for a long moment. Then, she asked, "Why do you want to be a queen, Fabiana?"

"So that I can make things right," I replied.

Perhaps the teacher understood that I was observing my surroundings and surveying the violence and threats. I knew innocent lives were in danger, and it affected how I viewed the world. Still, she might have wanted to avoid impractical daydreaming on my part, as she answered, "You cannot become a queen." She went on to list the reasons why it would not work.

Then, she continued, "What else do you want to be?"

"A lawyer," I said.

"Why?" she asked again.

"For the same reasons," I stated.

Becoming a lawyer seemed like a natural fit for me. I was confident and self-assured, and I had witnessed high-level conversations during my kindergarten years. As the country of Argentina changed, I saw an opportunity to add value there. In addition, school came easily to me. I have always had a sharp memory, and I could speak in a clear way to portray my position.

MOVING TO THE UNITED STATES

Despite my plan to stay in Argentina and work as a lawyer there, my father saw the value of gaining experience at other universities. He said to me, "Let's go to the United States, and you can apply. Once you get into a university, you can try it for six months, and then we can talk about it." I had already gained the title of a lawyer in Argentina. My father wanted me to get a master's degree from a college in a different country.

Complicating the plan was the fact that I was involved in a pretty serious relationship. My boyfriend lived in Argentina with no plans of leaving. Like me, he was part of a political family. His family belonged to the same political party as mine. It seemed we would continue together, and everything, both personally and professionally, would work out fine for us.

Even though I had my interests in staying in Argentina, I could see the insight in my father's approach. He wanted me to be the best I could, and for me, that would involve picking up further education from the United States. I agreed that we would travel to the United States and tour possible options. I would then apply and, after getting accepted, study for six months at the place. Then, I would talk to my father about coming home.

After making the agreement with my father, I had to break the news to my boyfriend's family. When they heard of my plan, they had different ideas. They didn't see the opportunities that could come from the arrangement. Instead, they felt it could cause us to drift apart.

To convey their feelings about me going to the United States, my boyfriend's family organized a very formal, beautiful lunch. Both of our families were in attendance. My parents sat down alongside the parents of my boyfriend. After exchanging polite conversation, his mother said, "You know … it is the woman who follows the man, not the man who follows the woman. We are not in agreement with Fabiana going to the United States."

I stood up from the table and said, "Well, I'm so sorry you feel like that. I have a solution for it." I paused and then went on, "Find yourself a new girlfriend. That's the solution."

As you can likely picture, this caused a bit of a stir. My mother wanted to talk further about the matter and the possibilities. She didn't want to lose the relationship with the other family either. My father, however, supported my standing. Pulling me aside, he said, "You're doing the right thing, Fabiana."

When that lunch ended, I knew very well that my life was about to undergo some significant changes. Just how large they would be, I may not have foreseen. I would head to the United States, and in addition to studying there, I would build my life and start a family.

STARTING IN COLORADO

I applied to several universities, and among the acceptance letters I received, I was also offered scholarships. One of these came from UCLA (University of California, Los Angeles). I thought it was a perfect solution, as I could study for six months and wouldn't have to pay for it. Then, I could go home to Argentina to make a difference in the country where I was born.

While I was ready to go to UCLA, my father once more had a different plan. He was a visionary, and it came through as he surveyed the university scene in the United States. He wanted me to try out a different school there first, to help me gain some experience so I could perform well at UCLA. "You don't know how it is to study in the US," he pointed out. "You should attend a different university and take a few classes just to understand how the tests work and how people study." He wanted me to enter UCLA ready to compete with the other students there and not get bogged down trying to figure out how to do the homework or turn in an assignment.

As before, I could see his reasoning, and we settled on a different university to begin. I enrolled in the University of Colorado Boulder and signed up for several classes. I would stay there for a semester and then go on to UCLA. I would also work as a ski instructor while I was there, which was great, because I loved skiing.

ADAPTING TO A NEW LIFE

With the plan set, my father took me up to the University of Colorado Boulder and helped me get settled in my new living quarters. He found me an apartment where I could stay, and once everything was in place, it was time for him to go back to Argentina. I would be on my own for the first time ever in my life. Prior to that moment, I had always been with family members. We had house personnel and a support system who had cared for myself and my sister.

I still remember the first night in my apartment after my father left. I sat on the floor and ate three Milky Ways. I felt an enormous weight on my shoulders. I had never cooked a meal before in my life. I had never made my bed or cleaned a room. I was coming from a very different environment, from a place where there were maids, gardeners, and cooks in our everyday lives. It was part of a system in which everyone played a role, and those that cared for us were considered like family, especially considering the tight security we had lived through together for so many years.

In this new setting, I would have to learn to do things on my own.

The next morning, from the new apartment, I called my nanny. I asked her, "How do I make the bed like at home?"

She said, "Oh, at home, baby (her term of endearment for me), we starch your sheets. So just pull hard."

I did the best I could, but it wasn't the same. After about three days, I realized other things that went beyond the initial differences I had noticed. In Argentina, the garbage was always taken out for us by our staff. At my new place, it just kept stacking up. No one was coming by asking for it.

I decided to ask my neighbors about it. I went to the place next door and knocked. There were three boys living there. When they opened the door, I asked, "Who picks up the garbage?"

The three of them just looked at each other. Then, they looked at me with confusion on their faces. Finally, one of them said, "What do you mean?"

I explained, "I have garbage in the house … Who's coming to pick it up?"

Another of the boys answered, "You take it to the dumpster."

"What's a dumpster?"

At this point, their expressions became dumbfounded. Then, they realized I really had no idea what a dumpster was and no concept of taking out the garbage on my own. "We'll help you," they said. And they did. They showed me the dumpster and helped me take out the trash.

From then on, I knew exactly where to put the garbage whenever the bin was ready to be emptied. While I missed the help and the people whom I saw every day in Argentina, there was also a sense of independence that came with taking care of things on my own. I was learning to live in a new place, step by step, and every day, I made progress.

In fact, this new independence soon overtook those initial moments of isolation. I soon realized that in the apartment, there was an answering machine. I had never had access to an answering machine of my own before. I was so excited that I could leave a message for anyone who called. For the first recording of my voice into the machine, I practiced for hours. I can still remember saying "This is Fabiana," in practically every tone possible—from friendly to even businesslike. I settled on one which I thought sounded fun and even a bit sultry.

However, this initial excitement was short lived. I faced a series of ups and downs during those initial months as a university student. Not long after I set up the answering machine, I started getting a series of odd callers. At first, an individual would call, and as soon as the machine picked up, they would hang up. Then, after calling and waiting for the recording to start, they would simply breathe into the line. This continued until I received a truly terrifying message. The recording of the person came through: "We're gonna get you tonight."

I heard the message at night, after coming home to my apartment, and I was horrified. I had lived through kidnapping attempts in a country where violence reigned for years. My mind immediately raced to the bad outcomes that could follow a call like this. I quickly called my father and explained what had happened.

"Fabiana, stop crying," he said. "I cannot understand you like this."

I tried to calm down so I could clearly explain that I thought I was about to be kidnapped.

Instead of responding right away, he continued, "Let's not wake up your mom." He had been next to her in the bedroom, and now, he moved into a corridor of our home in Argentina, where there was another phone in the wall he could pick up.

After switching to a different phone, he said, "Let me listen to the message."

I played it for him. After hearing it, he said, "It's not serious. You cannot be so worried about something that cannot be true because it makes no sense."

"What?!" What was going on?

He went on to say again, "It's not serious. It's not people from Argentina. They are not after you, because the target is me. And I'll tell you why."

My father spent the next thirty minutes giving me a history lesson and laying out the reasons why he thought I was not in any danger. He made it clear that anyone who might want to harm our family would first look for him, rather than his daughter who was living abroad.

Once I was able to breathe normally, my father went on to give recommendations for next steps. "If I were you," he said, "I would go to your friends next door. Then I would call the police and find out who is behind the calls. There has to be a reasonable explanation."

I took his word, and we ended our conversation. Then, I went to my neighbor's place, the unit that had three guys living in it. One of them, Peter, answered the door when I knocked. I explained my situation, and they agreed to let me stay there. I locked myself in the room that night.

Later, in looking into the calls, we learned it was in fact a series of prank calls. Some kids had apparently enjoyed listening to my voice (which at the time still had my racy recording on the machine!). They thought it was funny and kept calling to hear it. Now, I might add that saying "We're gonna get you tonight" was perhaps a poor choice of words on their end. But the fact was that my history and upbringing strongly influenced how I reacted.

That answering machine and the messages left on it were one of the first frightening episodes I had during my new life of independence. The ride was taking me up and down, but overall, I appreciated the chance to be in different contexts. As I learned, the prank caller in the United States was not targeting me in particular. My reaction was based on the experiences I had in Argentina. The experience turned out to be a good exercise. It allowed me to see how there can be different explanations, depending on the background of the individuals and the setting. It helped me see the importance of reacting in a way that is in tune with your environment.

Also, I changed my voicemail after that!

MOVING ON TO UCLA

After my time in Colorado, I settled in to pursue the goal my father had laid out. I would spend the rest of my six months in the United States studying at UCLA. There I enrolled in a master's program in international law with a concentration in environmental law.

The subject of the environment was especially meaningful to me because of what it represented for my home country. During those years, we were beginning to see the negative effects of ozone depleting substances in Argentina. The "hole" in the atmosphere above Antarctica had begun to expand. Argentina's positioning near Antarctica meant it was one of the first places to experience these consequences. Ushuaia, the capital of Tierra del Fuego, is approximately seven hundred miles from Port Lockroy, Antarctica.[4]

This meant that Argentina was receiving stronger ultraviolet rays than before, increasing the risk of conditions such as skin cancer and cataracts. Other countries were pointing to Argentina and talking about reducing the use of contaminants like chlorofluorocarbons (CFCs). However, I knew based on research that Argentina was not among the top producers of CFCs. Other countries were generating more of these harmful substances, and Argentina was nearly

---

4   "Port of Ushuaia, Argentina to Port Lockroy, Antarctica," Ports.com, http://ports.com/
    sea-route/port-of-ushuaia,argentina/port-lockroy,antarctica/.

getting the effect of them due to its placement on the globe.[5] It was important to me to see what could be done at an international level to protect both Argentina and other countries that were experiencing the depletion of the ozone—or would be soon.

Still, when I started at UCLA, I believed I would be heading home after the six-month period ended. I would do whatever research I could and then take what I had learned back home. After all, I had family and friends there and a whole life of things that were familiar to me. Moreover, my family had worked so hard for the country to become a democracy. It had taken so long, and now that they had achieved it, I felt far away. I wanted to be a part of it. I knew my sister, mother, and father were going to amazing social gatherings without me. They were eating meals that I missed, surrounded by faces I knew, loved, and missed.

In my head, my father's words echoed, "Six months." I decided I could do anything for six months. Plus, we had made an agreement. And my whole purpose for being a lawyer stemmed from my desire to make a difference. So maybe by living in a new place and studying there I could pick up some strategies to create a positive impact for others. Thus, I stayed.

At UCLA, my father rented an apartment where I could live. I remember the duration of the lease was one year. I told him, "We said six months."

He said, "That was the only option. There are only one-year leases available. Don't worry about it. At the six-month mark, you're free to come back."

---

5   "Fight against the Clock to Close the Hole in the Ozone Layer," World Bank, September 23, 2014, https://www.worldbank.org/en/news/feature/2014/09/23/lucha-tiempo-cerrar-agujero-capa-ozono-latinoamerica.

With that in mind, I started the classes at UCLA. Equipped with my previous experience and still enjoying the chance to learn how to live on my own, I soon found myself excelling. School was going great, and I was making new connections. By month three, I was nearly flying. "I want to see how this ends," I thought to myself.

At month four, I called my father and said, "I'm finishing. I'm going to stay."

"I knew it," he said.

My drive and ambition seemed to be like his. I didn't want to fail, and that energized me to give my very best. I wanted to see what I could achieve, and what I could accomplish. Through the classes and new circles, I was beginning to see that I really could make a difference—and I didn't need to race home to Argentina to do that.

FORMING NEW RELATIONSHIPS

Based on my determination to succeed (and high motivation because I didn't want to fail), I stayed longer than the initial six months. I wanted to complete the master's program in international law at UCLA. The people I met during this journey left a significant impression on me. Many helped me continue to adapt to everyday life in the United States. I formed new friendships, while taking care to maintain my connections to family and loved ones in Argentina.

Growing up in Latin America, I had learned strong social skills and knew how to follow formalities at events. I was very aware of how to act in different settings there. That said, I didn't know as much about social engagements in the United States. When one of my new connections through UCLA invited me to a wedding, I was unaware of the rules. I didn't know the proper protocol to follow.

So, I called my mom. "I've been invited to a wedding," I began. She jumped in immediately and shared her advice.

"Get a dress," she said. "Get your hair done and bring a gift." This was the typical approach for weddings in Argentina, and I figured it would be a good plan to try out for my first big social event in the United States.

I did all the preparations per my mom's instructions and showed up at the door on the day I thought had been indicated on the invitation. The address was a home, where I thought the wedding would take place. As I looked around, however, I thought everything seemed quiet.

Perhaps too quiet.

When the family opened the door, they looked at me curiously. "I'm here for the wedding," I said.

"You're a week early," they replied.

"Oh—"

"Do come in," they insisted. Seeing my dress and hair   I was obviously done up for an event—or simply because they wanted to, they insisted that I stay. They were having a family lunch and quickly found me a place.

I decided to stay and used the manners and formalities I had learned in Argentina. I was seated by an older gentleman for the meal. He asked me about my activities in the United States, and I explained that I was focused on writing my graduate thesis at UCLA, which was on the ozone depletion and global warming.

After listening to me, he asked, "Do you know who I am?"

"Maybe the uncle ... or the grandfather ...," I started.

"The uncle," he clarified. Then, he added that he was also an executive of the NASA Jet Propulsion Laboratory (JPL) in California. He shared that they happened to have a satellite looking at the ozone layers at that time. "Would you like to come on Monday to see?" he asked.

I was astounded. It was a huge opportunity. To be able to get images to use in my thesis would be highly useful. I finished the meal with the family and took the uncle up on his offer to visit the laboratory. The following week, I went in and looked at the images. The staff helped me download the best pictures, and I used them in my thesis work.

Had I not entered the residence when I arrived a week early for the wedding, I would have missed out on meeting the uncle. And if I hadn't used my social skills to have a conversation, I would never have learned about the images related to my project. Being able to use my social skills and connect with people led to doors being opened. It also helped me continue to adapt and feel at home in the United States little by little.

ANOTHER SIX-MONTH RULE

As agreed with my father, I finished the master's program at UCLA. I completed my thesis on environmental law, which thoroughly covered the ozone depletion and the effects in Argentina, along with what could be done at an international level to increase protection and reduce emissions. I was able to get very high grades and made some great connections along the way (including the executive of the NASA JPL in California and many others). It was natural for me to network with leaders and influencers; after all, I had been doing it since I was a child in Argentina.

Perhaps for these reasons, I was offered an amazing job immediately after completing the master's degree. The opportunity was for a law firm and seemed like a great fit, but it also gave me pause. I had been thinking of going back to Argentina after my studies were complete. Being employed in the United States would be a very different direction.

In addition, I hadn't fully expected to have the opportunity. I had been studying on a visa which allowed me to finish my education and then work for one year. Many companies did not hire or recruit individuals in my position. After one year, if we were unable to legally stay, we would leave the country. That would be considered a loss by most organizations. Given this, I was quite surprised when the law firm asked me to come to work for them.

I called my father and told him of the development. "You know, I wanted to go back," I said after sharing the news of the job offer.

He didn't agree with me. "Don't collect regrets," he said. "You don't want to look back and ask yourself what it would have been like to work in the US."

His point carried weight, as I didn't know if I would be offered an opportunity to work there again. He continued, "You cannot really make an informed decision unless you work for six months first. So, you should work for six months, and then you'll have all the elements you need to make an informed decision."

That was more than thirty years ago. In a nutshell, I took the job and went on to become legally able to stay in the United States. I got married, had a family, and raised my children all within its borders.

As hard as I know it was for my father to encourage me to try the job for six months, he really wanted me to be the best I could. Living in the United States, I grew familiar with a judicial system that I saw I could work in. For me, it's always been about trying to do the right things, to make a difference, to create equality, and to leave an impact. I realized I could carry out those values in the United States. Ultimately, those were the reasons that motivated me to stay. I missed my family and Argentina, but I also knew that others back home would continue to work for their values there. I could find ways to make things right in the United States and eventually on a global scale as well.

THE BENEFITS OF A LONG-TERM APPROACH

I took those lessons of waiting for six months before making a decision to heart. This long-term and calculated outlook has helped me throughout my personal life and career. Years after completing the graduate program at UCLA, when facing a difficult situation, I would find myself thinking of six months. I would sit down and say to myself, "You cannot change the dark. You can only bring light, at least to those around you … so what's your plan?" Then, I would write it out. I would list the actions I would take. I would note what I could control, which often included my emotions and my environment. This simple exercise gave me so much power. It helped me clarify my thoughts and avoid making fast, irrational decisions.

These days, I encourage others to do the same. Having a six-month rule can be particularly helpful at work, especially if you're thinking about switching jobs or positions. In recent years, record numbers of Americans have quit their jobs. Many cite reasons such as low pay, no opportunities to advance, or feeling disrespected by others.[6] If you're in a position that you would like to leave, it could be beneficial to take some time to write down your reasons. Consider the potential effects of your actions. You might also set a timeline for deciding.

Carrying out this exercise could lead you to take additional steps. You might gather more information, such as asking coworkers or a higher-up about your options. You could check for opportunities you might have missed, such as seeing if you can negotiate your salary or benefits or take on different responsibilities that you would enjoy.

---

6   Kim Parker and Juliana Menasce Horowitz, "Majority of Workers Who Quit a Job in 2021 Cite Low Pay, No Opportunities for Advancement, Feeling Disrespected," Pew Research Center, March 9, 2022, https://www.pewresearch.org/short-reads/2022/03/09/majority-of-workers-who-quit-a-job-in-2021-cite-low-pay-no-opportunities-for-advancement-feeling-disrespected/.

If you take a long-term approach, rather than making an abrupt decision, you could be happier with the eventual outcome. You'll at least know you did all you could to get as many facts as possible to move forward with confidence.

Taking a long-term approach could help you be patient as you acquire new capabilities, too. As new technologies continue to roll in, it may be necessary to spend time learning a technique or process that is very different than what you've done in the past. My friend and former boss Andrew Oxtoby, former CEO of Aimmune, identified the value in being willing to adapt, even if things aren't easy right away. "I think that whenever you embrace something new, whether it's learning a new language, trying a new skill, or taking a new approach in the work environment, you probably aren't going to do it very well," he explained. "One of the things that will be necessary going forward is enough humility to put yourself in a position where you're not going to be perfect." Over time, if you're persistent, you'll be able to adjust. You might even go on to teach others what you've learned.

KNOWING WHEN TO WALK

While I tend to advocate for a six-month rule, I also understand that there are situations when less time is needed. You never want to compromise your integrity or values. If you're working in an environment that is carrying out actions you feel are not right, it may be best to walk away. It could be crucial to your overall well-being.

I know this because I've done it! I've left positions that didn't align with my value, even if I didn't have an open door waiting for me to walk through. What I found by going through experiences like this is that there will always be another day. You can wake up and work toward a better future, find a different job that fits your values, and land in a place where you can maintain your integrity and dignity. As I like to tell others, "There might be times in your life when you have to walk away, but for everything else, the six-month rule is great. And MasterCard."

As a leader, there are different strategies to take for every situation. You need to know which one to use and then apply it. This is true in both business and life. As Kenny Rogers sings, "You've got to know when to hold 'em, when to fold 'em, know when to walk away, and know when to run."[7]

TEACHING OTHERS THE SIX-MONTH RULE

Decades after graduating from UCLA, when I had three children, a husband, and a career that sent me around the world, our family faced some moves. My work would often take us to new places within the United States. We would have to find a new home, different schools for the children, and adjust to the surrounding community.

One time, shortly after moving to California, I realized my oldest son, Maximo, was not doing well in school. He was a freshman in high school and was struggling in certain aspects to adapt academically. I looked through his grades and saw they were a disaster. He was failing a class, and his scores in other subjects were low, too.

I sat down with him to address the matter. "I'll give you six months," I told him. "This is the six-month rule. You have that amount of time to improve your grades. I want to see all As and Bs. If they don't reach that level, I will implement a plan of my own. And chances are, you won't like it."

Six months later, we revisited Maximo's grades. By then, it was December—right in the middle of the school year. The grades had not gone up. They continued to be a disaster.

---

7   Kenny Rogers, "The Gambler," SongFacts, https://www.songfacts.com/lyrics/kenny-rogers/the-gambler.

True to my word, I put my own plan into action. I walked my son to a new school and enrolled him there. It was a reputable, all-boys school. I had researched the place and thought it would be a good fit for him.

Maximo wasn't sure. "It's the middle of the year," he protested.

"I thought I was clear about the six months," I replied. "It just happens to be December."

Though he wasn't necessarily thrilled about the change, looking back it turned out to be the best decision ever. His grades improved, and he did well for the rest of his high school years. He even went on to continue his education and go to law school.

The change wasn't easy, and it took time. Looking back, it was the right thing to have a six-month rule. It gave him time to improve his grades. It also set an end date when a different action could be taken. If I hadn't done anything, his grades might not have improved. By having a careful, calculated approach, I also showed him steps he can now take in his own life and career.

Even now, as I'm surrounded by family, my sister Valeria who came two years after me to the United States, and her family, I haven't forgotten what it was like to be a newcomer. I remember crying myself to sleep so many nights because everything was very foreign, and my support system was so far away. I wasn't used to the types of challenges I faced during those initial months and years. I missed my deep friendships in Argentina, my tribe, my earliest supporters, family and friends like Cris Dolo, I. Vicki S., and Vero E., and las Margaritas from SMS, the school I attended. I had formed such strong bonds with people there, and we had grown together during intense years of unrest and violence. These loved ones, whom I considered my chosen sisters and who knew me better than anyone else, were thousands of miles away. My biological sister was, too. They were living a very different life than me.

However, I also recognize that I was able to adapt and grow a career in the United States. I didn't go on to work for multinational companies without a strong work ethic, strength, perseverance, and courage. I had to draw on those qualities to make it work.

I chose to put in the effort, find a way, and reach the finish line. These days, as I tell my children, I always recognize that there is an option to quit. When we face difficult situations, we can choose to give up. But deciding to stay and persevere, rather than walking away, is what truly defines who you are. It's not about the outcome—it's about the journey. And I choose, time and again, to be a warrior. I hope you do, too.

KEY TAKEAWAYS

- The six-month rule for decision-making can help you gather more information and reflect on the impact of your choices.
- Embracing new experiences can help you grow and mature and gain a deeper understanding of other cultures and places.
- There may be times when you need to walk away from a situation to preserve your integrity and values, even if there isn't a clear path forward.
- Pushing yourself to adapt and grow can lead to a sense of fulfillment, and you can be proud of being a warrior.

CHAPTER 4

THE RELOCATION

After I finished my education in the United States and decided to stay, I shifted into the next phase of my life. This included my career path, and it started out strong. I was sought after for my grades, ability to present myself, and the extensive background I had. I was able to speak more than one language, carry out negotiations seamlessly with high-level executives and positions of influence, and most of all, I enjoyed a challenge.

Early in my career, I was hired by a company for a position I was excited about. Shortly after, I had an opportunity to move to a new location. I could still work for the company, but it would be at a different branch.

I wanted to take the opportunity, so we began negotiating for a relocation package. In reviewing my situation, I knew I didn't have a long history with the company. However, it was important for me to have a future with the firm, so I wanted the negotiation to go well.

To prepare for the move, I looked over what it would cost and came up with a figure of $5,000. I asked the company for that amount to cover my relocation expenses. The request was accepted.

I remember when I got the approval for the funding, I thought it was more than enough. I was thrilled to have a job and be given a new opportunity. The negotiation process had gone smoothly, and I felt I was building good relationships at the company.

Then, shortly after my $5,000 was approved, I learned that a man I knew at the same company also received a relocation package. Like me, he had carried out negotiations for it. When he came to the table, he had asked the company for $50,000. (This was thirty years ago, so you can imagine the difference! In today's dollars, that $50,000 would be over $115,000.[8] In contrast, my $5,000 would be equivalent to about $13,500.[9]) Besides that amount in cash, he requested a long list of extras. These included covering the cost of his club fees to paying the moving expenses for his dog.

In the end, I got the $5,000 I requested. And he got $50,000 plus the other amenities. We both moved. While our circumstances and level of experience could have had an impact on the company's decision on how much to give, the fact remained that we both asked for an amount and received it.

The experience was an important one in my career. It made me recognize that I needed to get much better at playing the negotiating game and advocating for myself. I wanted to know my worth and be ready to command a high price. I worked hard and always strived to make a difference. It would be important to help companies see the

---

8   "The Value of $50,000 from 1990 to 2024," Carbon Collective, https://tools.carboncollective.co/inflation/us/1990/50000/#:~:text=%2450%2C000%20in%201990%20has%20the,was%20%2D0.72%25%20per%20year.

9   Ibid.

value I could bring to their workplace, too. And if I didn't ask for it, no one else would step in and do it for me.

Look around at your own life and you'll see negotiations taking place all over. They are often part of a salary package for a new job or discussions surrounding a promotion. You might negotiate when buying a larger item like a car or getting a bid for a home renovation. In families, negotiations are often part of everyday conversations. What show will be watched after dinner? Who will plan out the next vacation? How will a broken bike get repaired? All these involve at least two parties, and each side comes with a set of interests and values. Sorting through the options and finding a solution is a process that can end well—or it can lead to heated arguments, suboptimal outcomes, and even broken relationships.

Being a leader includes negotiating well, with respect to others, and in a way that is reasonable. To improve your chances, you need to get in the best position possible. This all starts with knowing your worth. You can come well prepared, understand what you're bringing to the table, know how it will benefit the other party, and be ready to walk if needed. In my personal life and work, putting these strategies into place has resulted in positive outcomes personally and professionally, strong relationships with my kids, and the satisfaction that comes from knowing my worth—and being able to communicate it.

As you read on, take some time to reflect on your own negotiations. Perhaps you've had outcomes that were similar to my $5,000 check and want to get better solutions. Maybe you're looking to get a promotion at work and secure certain benefits that are important to you. Or you might be hoping to convince a contractor to accept your bid, have a well-run household, or enjoy meals with loved ones. All these tactics will help you do those and more. It all starts by looking within and learning to stand up for yourself in the right way at the right time.

HONOR YOURSELF

There is nothing more beautiful than having high self-esteem. It shows you are aware of your skills and abilities. You know where you've come from and where you're going. If you believe that you are doing the right things for the right reasons, this knowledge is extremely powerful. It will motivate you to stand up for yourself and live out your values. All of these speak to honoring yourself.

In addition, confidence is very attractive. People often admire individuals who come across as self-assured. However, there's a fine line between being confident and arrogant. While it's important to know your self-worth, you can communicate it without disregarding other people's capabilities. You don't have to put anybody down to feel strong about what you are able to contribute.

This includes knowing your boundaries. If you're true to yourself and listen to your intuition, you'll know what you can accept. You'll be aware of the lines you're not willing to cross. If a negotiation reaches a point that doesn't align with your values, you'll be able to walk away with the assurance that you're doing what's best.

When I take on a new position, during the negotiating process, I'm often asked, "How much do you want to make?" Rather than giving a figure or range, I like to pose a question. I generally respond, "How much is this position worth to you?" This creates a certain amount of exposure. It reveals how the company views the position compared to others. For instance, if the offer I'm given for a leadership position is the same amount as what other executives on the leadership team are receiving, it will typically mean the position is very important to them.

Now, I work for more than money, which we'll cover later, but the point is that this discussion opens the door to new possibilities. I can look at the compensation they offer for the position, and if I feel it is fair, I can share with them what I'm able to do. This often leads to a reasonable outcome, whereas if I merely state a figure when asked what I want to make, I could be missing out on compensation for the position that the company feels is appropriate.

VALUE YOUR LIFE

When I was living in Argentina with my family, before coming to the United States, my father insisted I learn to look out for myself. He wanted me to learn how to value myself and my life. He knew the importance of honoring yourself. He made me take defensive driving training so I could be prepared for what might happen on the road. If I faced a threat from another person or vehicle or turned a corner and drove into a violent situation, he wanted me to know what to do.

In a similar way, he made me learn how to shoot a gun. He told me, "Nobody is going to value your life more than you do. Bodyguards have a job, and they are good at it. But you need to value your life more than anyone and be willing to fight for it." Thanks to his influence, I became able to defend myself and had a plan for what steps to take if the unexpected occurred.

Even if you haven't lived in a war zone or tense neighborhood, you can think through what's important to you. Consider what you're willing to do to survive. Creating a plan will help you be prepared and make the right decisions if something does happen.

This exercise can be worthwhile in case of an emergency. For instance, going to school or the mall on a regular day might seem completely risk-free. Keep in mind, however, that dangerous situations can arise quickly (think of the headlines relating to shootings in these places). What would you do if someone walked in with a gun? How would you advise your loved ones to act if they face a threat in a public setting? In my case, I've had discussions with my children on what to do in a life-threating event. They know how they would act, where they would go, and who they would try to contact. This gives them greater confidence in themselves and increases their ability to make smart moves under pressure.

When I was younger, some of my friends had boyfriends, and they valued them highly. They even told their boyfriends, "I love you so much that I would die for you." I remember hearing these phrases and thinking about my own priorities. For me, my three kids are the only individuals in the world that I would die for. Everybody else needs to get in line.

BE CLEAR ON WHAT YOU WANT

Before you enter a negotiation, think through what you're willing to receive. Maybe for a new job, you say, "I really need a signing bonus." Then, consider what else you might be happy with. For instance, what if the company doesn't offer you a signing bonus but gives you a different benefit? Perhaps the executives lay out a figure that you'll receive after you've worked for the company for a certain time. If you only think about the signing bonus, you could be limiting yourself. You might turn down other options that could lead to good outcomes, too.

In my case, rather than focusing on the signing bonus, I generally look for equity compensation. This is non-cash pay that is offered to employees which allows them to become part of the ownership of the company. It could include stock options and performance shares if certain objectives are met. As a leader in an organization, if you're paid in equity, you'll have the chance to direct some areas. You can play a role, to a certain extent, in how the company performs. There's also usually a layer of protection in case something happens that could impact your options or shares. For instance, you might have a change-in-control agreement, which would provide payouts if the company is acquired and your position gets eliminated in the process. For me, I'd rather get paid in equity, because I know that I can demonstrate what I'm worth and what I can do, and I can influence an outcome.

That said, for me, it's important to work for reasons that go beyond salary and benefits. There could be opportunities to grow personally and professionally. There might be a chance to take on a new job where you'll be able to make a difference. I always look for an environment where people have high integrity. It could be beneficial to work with highly respected people and learn from them.

Generally speaking, in a negotiation, you cannot have it all. The solution must be fair and equitable. So, set aside time to lay out what would work for you. Ask yourself what you're willing to compromise on and where you will be less flexible. Early in my career, whenever I was preparing to negotiate a contract for a company as their attorney, I would carefully read through all the clauses listed. Then, I would look for additional ones we could add that the other party might view as beneficial. I would also try to change existing clauses so they would favor the other party. I would outline which terms could not be changed. That way, I was improving my chances of getting what I wanted. The other party would feel understood and respected, based on the additional and modified clauses we offered, and our company would be able to keep what was important to it as well.

COME PREPARED

I always tell my children that if they are going to have a discussion with me, they should come prepared. I will want to hear well-thought-out points that support their opinion or request. For instance, not long ago, one of my kids asked for the keys to my convertible instead of their own car to go to school. It was shortly before a holiday season, and I knew the kids were anxious to be on break. I asked, "Why should I give you the keys to my car?"

After a couple of attempts that didn't entice me, my child explained that it was the last day of school before vacation. They wanted to put the top down and enjoy the warm weather while listening to music. They wanted to arrive at school feeling ready for their last classes.

In the end, I agreed and let them borrow my car. The experience proved to be a good teaching moment. You need to know who you're talking to and what will motivate them. While I might not give out keys if a child says they are feeling lazy and don't want to find their own set of keys(!), I will support an attitude that wants to celebrate life and be open to learning.

The same holds true when preparing for a job interview. You'll want to do the research beforehand and know who will be at the meeting. What salaries are others in your peer group making? How are similar positions being compensated? What are the company's needs? What is the culture like and how are employees treated? What motivates the individuals who are hiring? What are they looking for? Finding the answers to these questions could put you in a better position to have a conversation that leads to an offer.

Practice what you'll say beforehand as well. If you are negotiating a new job, and you want a signing bonus of $100,000, it might not be the best approach to say, "I need $100,000 as a starting point." You could end up in an inflexible position. What if the company is unable to give a $100,000 signing bonus? Suppose they offer you $50,000? You might say, "I understand you can only give me a signing bonus of $50,000 now. But how about I get an additional bonus a year from now if I meet these objectives?" You could explain what you plan to accomplish and show that you're willing to work for results.

DRAW ON YOUR EXPERIENCES

Remember that you're unique, and your background could be used to your advantage. Maybe you didn't go to an Ivy League school, or perhaps you grew up in a low-income area with little access to education. Suppose you had to work while going to school to support your family. Or that you moved frequently as a child and didn't have a chance to settle in one place.

Whatever it is, if you got through a hardship and grew from it, that shows a sign of leadership. It tells others that you are resilient. Those experiences can make you incredibly strong, courageous, and persistent. They also put you in a place where you can empathize with others. Coworkers might feel more comfortable around you because they can relate to your background and respect you for how far you've come. You might even be compelled to reach out to the community and find ways to help others who are going through similar experiences that you had when you were younger.

If you're looking at a possible job and see that the company has a list of requirements for the position, compare it to your own background. You might be able to demonstrate that you have the experience and skills, even if they don't completely match with what is stated on paper. That's because there's more to just a résumé for everyone—we all have histories and unique abilities that we can apply to a situation.

That's what happened when I interviewed Brenda Crabtree, now director of compliance at a global biopharmaceutical company. She didn't have years of compliance experience to draw from, even though she was applying for a position in compliance. Still, she really wanted the opportunity and laid out her experiences that she had in other areas as well as her skill set. I noticed that she had been in the Navy as an officer. Because I'm married to a veteran, I know the discipline and work ethic that these servicemembers can bring to the table. I hired her on the spot, and she was fabulous at the position—just as I knew she would be.

GATHER FEEDBACK

To improve your negotiating skills, look for input from others, including mentors, peers, and those who report to you. For me, I even get feedback from my children. They have attended some lectures and presentations and have seen me as I confronted complex issues and how I handled them. They've shared their feedback with me.

In one case, I was asked to be the opening speaker at a large women's leadership conference. I had been invited by my good friend Liz Archibald—someone I count on in my inner circle. She is a fellow warrior with a gift for communication, and I value our friendship. Although I consider myself a strong speaker, she provided feedback that made my presentations even more impactful and powerful. This shows how you can listen to those you trust and who are experts in their field—they can help you move up another level.

My son, who is now a lawyer himself, was scheduled to attend the conference. When he realized I was the starting presenter and he would be there, he said, "Don't mention my name, Mom."

I replied, "By now you should know, I say what I want to say, how I want to say it, so …"

The day of the conference arrived, and my presentation topic was on the future of compliance. At the event, there were about five hundred in attendance. During the talk, when asked what the future of compliance is, I said, "The future of compliance is sitting among you. And it's my son. He started hearing these concepts when he was a baby, and the conversation hasn't changed much. It's about integrity, about doing the right thing, and about making a difference."

I didn't mention my son's name or his workplace. He was seated in the audience, though, and other attendees looked around to try to spot him. After the event, many found him. We share the same last name, so it wasn't too hard to discover who he was.

When it was over, I connected with my son to get feedback on the conference. He said, "Mom, I have never been more popular. People kept coming up to me and asking if I was your son!" He ended up appreciating the association, and we had a laugh over the experience.

Then, I asked what he thought of the presentation. He paused and then said, "You're different."

"What makes me different?"

"You're passionate, and people are compelled to listen to you. But it's not just that … The others knew the textbook and theory of compliance, but you have been part of the game, and it showed."

It was good feedback, and I do truly believe you have to learn how the game is played and get in there to play. Throughout my career, I have taken opportunities that would help me gain new experiences and be part of the decisions. I know I can influence outcomes, and at the conference, I had come across as confident and knowledgeable.

STAY BALANCED

Once you know what you can bring to the table at a negotiation, think about what you want, and do your research, you'll be ready to participate. Remember that during the discussion, your presentation is key. If the other parties perceive you as too demanding or upset, you might not get what you want. Emotional intelligence comes into play here, as you'll need to observe how others respond, listen to your intuition, and calmly explain your position.

Even if you get exactly what you want, the way you get it matters. Suppose you are scheduled for a performance review and are hoping to get more time off in the coming months. If you are condescending or don't listen to others during the negotiation, you could still end up getting the extra vacation days you request. However, the company might simply be granting it because they need you and don't have an immediate replacement. Later, it's possible they'll hire someone else to take your place. Or they could pass over you when it's promotion time and choose someone else who has a more balanced approach to negotiating.

At times, companies have hired me and given me an offer that I have accepted right away. I didn't even ask to negotiate. Instead, I have said, "I'll accept this now." I've explained that I know they are giving me what they think is best and because they want me for the position. I've also assured them that they've made the right decision by hiring me. Then, I've added that we can have a conversation to negotiate later, such as at bonus time.

This approach shows that I'm willing to leave the door open for future conversations. It also communicates to the company that I may be looking for more compensation later. After they've seen my performance and the results I've driven, they may be interested in negotiating both to reward me and to keep me in the position.

DON'T COMPARE YOURSELF TO OTHERS

It can be easy to look at what coworkers receive and wonder why you don't have it. I always point out, though, that you could only be seeing one aspect. You might not know the full story or reasoning behind the decisions. Even when I asked for $5,000 rather than $50,000 for a relocation, I used the experience as a lesson, rather than a point of comparison.

I remember working for a company that compensated me more in equity than cash at one point. Others in my peer group, however, were paid more in cash than equity. I didn't understand why my boss had made this decision and why I wasn't getting the same amount as others. I was even upset about it for a time. It didn't seem fair to me.

But about six months later, the company was bought by another company. This brought on many changes for the employees. Due to the change of control agreement that I had with the company, my equity was accelerated. The result was in my favor, and I received it by continuing with the company even when the compensation didn't seem fair at first.

CREATE OPEN CHANNELS OF COMMUNICATION

For a time, I had a very confrontational relationship with a coworker at a company where I was working. I had found out he was misusing a process to his advantage, and I found it upsetting. When it came up in discussion, however, he was unprofessional and even started name-calling.

I shared that I was willing to have different points of view, but we needed to treat each other with respect to solve the issue. When my boss learned of the situation, he asked me what I was going to do about it. I said, "Actually, I want to invite him to lunch. We'll go out once a week until we can talk about it and listen to each other."

My boss thought it was a genius idea. My coworker was outraged. Still, we went out to our first lunch date as planned. He brought a newspaper and started reading it at the table. I sat across from him and decided to make the lunch as long as possible. I made comments such as, "Oh wow, I never thought you could make salmon with rice like that!" He didn't respond.

When the meal came to an end, I said, "We'll meet next week. We'll see each other until we finally can talk." He gave me a cold look.

The next week, at the appointed lunch date, I asked, "Are we friends today?"

"Absolutely not."

The rest of the lunch carried on with his silence and my comments.

Still, we agreed to meet again. I wanted to get to the point where I would either have his respect or he would learn to work with me. Or, ideally, both. By the third lunch, he started talking. Over time, we found a way to discuss the issue in a reasonable, respectful way.

That experience helped me see that generally, heated disagreements don't advance the discussion. We must respect each other and find a working relationship. When this is done, we can better find a solution and move forward.

As I look back and think about that $5,000 relocation package, I also remember how I didn't have a longstanding relationship with the company at the time. In the moment, I felt it was more important for me to have a future with the company than to challenge the offer or ask for more. Had I come back in a very strong and unreasonable way and demanded more after I learned of the $50,000 package, I could have missed out on future opportunities. Those in authority might have thought I pushed too far, and they might not have offered me later promotions or bonuses. Instead, I was able to keep the relationship with the company. I also learned key lessons that I applied to later negotiations and had successful outcomes.

In the end, I moved happily. I was able to make a difference at the company. And later, I had the chance to show the contributions I had made after the relocation. More importantly, I had demonstrated that I was a team player, and that I was willing to accept offers in a reasonable, balanced approach.

Later in my career, I faced another relocation opportunity. This time, however, I was working for a company that wanted me to move, and I wasn't willing to transfer. They were paying me very well, but still I wanted to remain where I was. I told them, "I'll stay on until you find somebody that can relocate." So, I continued to work for the company, with the understanding that it wasn't a long-term arrangement. Once they found someone else, that person would take my place.

They looked for the right individual, and the process took some time. A year and a half later, they had found the person to take over my position. She connected with me and soon realized how much I was making. She was so shocked. She couldn't help herself when she asked, "How can somebody make that much? That's more than double what I make!"

I knew she was looking at me and recognizing that I was "Latino" and a woman. It must have seemed impossible for me to be compensated that much, due to my minority status. I just laughed and said, "Well, somebody has to do it. Why not me?"

But what I really meant, and she realized too, was that I was at the company for a reason. I was working to make a difference, and I had come to the table knowing my worth when they put me in the position. The company also highly valued my role and recognized I was working hard and had an education, experience, integrity, the ability to speak more than one language, and passion. All of that played a role in the compensation. And it showed how far I had come from my $5,000 relocation package negotiation.

As you think about your own negotiations in life and at work, don't get down about what's happened in the past. You can learn from any mistakes that were made. You can also draw on your background to show how you are unique and will bring valuable insight to the table.

Look at each negotiation as an opportunity to be respectful and build a relationship. Remember that you could get delayed benefits that are even better than what you could imagine today. Most of all, be confident and know your worth—and be ready to communicate it to others!

KEY TAKEAWAYS

- In negotiations, you'll want to maintain professionalism and work toward positive relationships that could keep the door open for future discussions.
- Understand the skills you bring to the table and know your worth. Be confident in your abilities and what you can contribute.
- Instead of focusing on what others have, advocate for your own needs and interests. Every situation is different, and your priorities might not be the same as what's important for others.
- Look to keep long-term relationships built on trust and credibility which can lead to future opportunities.

CHAPTER 5

EVERY SIGN TELLS A STORY

I used to have a law school professor who said there is no violent crime that happens without warning. If you think about it, there's always a sign. Sometimes, we might observe the red flags of danger but not listen to them or react to them. If we don't pay attention, we miss the warnings and might not take action to stop the crime from taking place.

You'll generally see that people who commit violent crimes have a certain personality type. They typically like to feel powerful. They often want to make people feel a certain way. These criminals will send out signals before becoming violent.

This became very apparent to me during a time when I worked on a project that covered rape victims. For the work, I interviewed a lot of women who had been raped. They talked to me about their experiences and shared many details.

The premise of the project was that there are no violent crimes that are unannounced. That held true in my discussions with these women. Every single person I spoke with told me that they had noticed something that was off before the crime took place.

During my conversations with these victims, I learned that these women typically had a feeling that something wasn't right before they were attacked. But they didn't know exactly what to do and weren't sure how to react. I heard comments such as, "After offering to carry my grocery bags to the door, he asked for a glass of water. He was standing outside the door, and I didn't want to lock the door while I was getting it. It would be like closing the door in his face, and he had just helped me carry up my groceries."

Now, because of my background of growing up in a corrupt and violent setting, I didn't have this same sense of uneasiness. It was logical for me to say, "In those types of situations, if you feel uncomfortable, you should just lock yourself up. When you do that, you're telling them, 'I'm on to you. It's not going to be easy.'"

That said, I recognize that not everyone has the same training that I do. But I have found in my work experience that awareness can be taught. You can learn to pick up on details and notice subtle differences. You can take the time to know who you're dealing with. Being surprised is not a good thing, no matter what the situation is.

If you learn to notice the signs and find the story behind them, you'll be able to do more than just avoid violent crimes. These skills transfer into corporate America, where spotting the small details that most overlook can make a big difference in a deal. If something makes you uncomfortable, you should act on it.

As you read through the following sections, think through your daily routines. Consider how you act as you carry out regular tasks and if you pay attention to your surroundings. Also think about how you feel and act when you are in a different setting, such as when you travel to a work conference or take a vacation. The strategies I share here will help you notice signs and find the story behind them. When you do, you can avoid negative circumstances, and you'll also be able to influence positive change.

BE AWARE OF YOUR STRESS LEVELS

We all have stressors in our life. It's what you do with them that determines the outcome. If you pay attention to what's happening, you can decide how you'll react. It starts with acknowledging what you're facing and being aware of your uneasiness. Then, you can decide what you will do with the stress.

As I've mentioned in previous chapters, when I came from Argentina to the United States, I faced many changes in my environment. In Argentina, I had grown up with people who took care of all my needs. Suddenly, in the United States, I had to do many things on my own. I learned to live in the new country and establish a career and household.

During my years in the United States, I have come across people with many different backgrounds and stories. Often, when we first meet, we have no idea what the other person has been through. In asking questions, we start to learn more and more. One time, when I was talking to someone who probably didn't fully understand my upbringing, they asked me, "How are you at taking risks?"

It was an innocent question, but I had to laugh as I thought of my risk-taking. I responded, "Well, I grew up in Argentina and came to live in this country ... What else do I need to do?"

All joking aside, one of the reasons I was able to grow up in Argentina during a difficult time and settle well in the United States was due to my ability to respond correctly to the stressors. Rather than get scared and indecisive, I was able to observe every situation.

Thanks to my father's teachings and example, I could manage the stress. I used it as motivation to adapt to new environments and learn from every experience.

My sister and I grew up being aware of everything that surrounded me, both big and small. Due to the critical settings we were in, where decisions could mean life or death, it was important to have as much data as possible at all times. That way, I could make the best decisions with the information I had and be confident in my choices.

After I moved to the United States, I kept connections with friends and family members in Argentina. When my sister Valeria moved to America a couple of years after me to pursue a different career, it was nice to have her closer, and we quickly realized that we both brought the same skill set to our lines of work. We are observant and socially aware. If we notice something seems amiss, we will act on it at the right time.

The same could be said of my closest friends from Argentina. We have recognized that even though we live in different locations, we are raising our kids with similar values. We often use the same phrases and the same examples. My background, together with how I raise my kids now, demonstrates that we can use stressors to our advantage. I don't regret my upbringing and think I'm better for it. I have high emotional intelligence; I know how to recognize my stress, to listen to it, and to use it to make decisions and take action.

WATCH FOR DETAILS

When I was a child in Argentina, we had to look for the reason behind every action. One time, in the middle of the night, the doorbell rang. It was 3:00 a.m., and it woke up the household. My whole family had been asleep—my father, mother, sister, and myself—and suddenly, we were all awake.

My father went to see what was happening. From outside, the person at the door said that they were bringing flowers to us. They were delivering an order in the middle of the night. This seemed out of place, to say the least. Not ready to open the door and face a potential threat outside, my father stayed inside. He said, "Leave them there."

But the delivery person insisted that we open the door. The conversation continued, and my sister, mother, and I went to hide. We were all feeling stressed. We knew that anything could happen based on the signs and what they could mean.

The delivery guy went on to explain from outside the door that he had been planning to bring the flowers earlier and had been delayed. There had been an accident, and he had to wait for it. Now, he had made it to the door and needed a signature to confirm receipt. If he went back to his workplace without it, he would get fired.

It was a reasonable explanation once he laid it out that way. Still, our hesitation to open the door had also been correct. We were living in a place where kidnappings could occur anywhere, and our family especially was threatened. We had to pay attention to the signs. At the same time, after listening to the story from the delivery man, we also recognized that it added up. Once we knew his reasonings and situation, our feelings of alarm subsided. My father's ability to stay calm and find the details had led to a solution that worked for everyone. The flowers were delivered, and the delivery person was able to get the signature.

SAFE ROUTINES

Part of paying attention to details involves setting up a plan. If you do something step by step and make it a routine, you can better notice when something is off. For unexpected events, you can decipher the cause and find a solution you're comfortable with.

In my case, as an adult, I draw on my training to be alert which started as a child. Whenever it's dark around me, I tend to be extra aware. Often, for crimes and violence, the night represents a time to do something that is wrong. A criminal might come for you when it's hard for you to see them approaching, or when you won't notice them entering a room you are in.

Every once in a while, in the place where I live, the power goes off (you've probably had something like this happen to you, too). One night, a storm raged around our home, tripping the power. Instantly, I was awake. And I woke up my husband, too.

He wasn't worried, but I wasn't ready to go back to sleep. I wanted to make sure I knew the source of the power outage. Was it for everyone? Had someone cut the power off to our house? My intuition knew that it could be due to several reasons. I got up and checked to see if other houses had also lost power. Soon, I learned that the whole neighborhood was without electricity. The storm had knocked something off, and we had to wait for the power to come back on. It was a reasonable explanation, and I also knew that it was worth investigating to make sure all was safe.

This process of checking the source of the issue, and not going back to sleep until I know the cause, is one of my safety routines that I rely on. In the same way, whenever I enter a hotel room, I have a pattern that I follow. I need to know right away where all the exits are. Before I lock myself in, I have to see where I could escape if needed. Once I know the exits, I look everywhere and make sure there are no warning signs anywhere. Then, I lock myself in. During my stay in the hotel room, nobody comes in for any reason unless I want them inside.

It may seem extreme or exaggerated, but I believe these are things that make me special. I have plans I can follow, and it helps me better detect when something isn't right. Then, I can investigate a situation before it gets out of control. I'm also able to calmly look for a cause and decide what to do based on the information I discover along the way.

Having the capability to stay calm and observe the situation gives you the upper hand. You'll be able to better assess the event and make a smart, calculated decision. You won't have to be overrun with anxiety or mixed feelings, which can lead to indecision or poor outcomes. Just think of what my former professor said about violent crimes. If you know to watch for the signs, and have high emotional intelligence, you'll be aware of the stressors—and be able to act on them in a way to protect yourself and your loved ones.

TRAIN YOURSELF TO SPOT WHAT'S DIFFERENT

Even if you grew up in a quiet suburb or remote village, there are steps you can take to increase your awareness. In corporate America, I have done various training programs at different companies to teach skills like survival in captivity and defensive driving. I've taught people what to do if you're ever working in a country and get pulled aside to be interrogated. The sessions cover topics like security, escape, being aware, and having a plan.

During one of my training programs, I took the team I was teaching to a restaurant, where we ate in a private dining room. I told them beforehand that the training would continue through the meal. I also reminded them that there are no coincidences. For men, as I always say, "If you think you are that good looking, think twice. Nobody's going to instantly fall in love with you." Many times, acts that seem unnatural or out of place are a sign that something under

75

the surface is wrong. I always warn people to be suspicious in these cases as well.

The restaurant was a Brazilian steakhouse, where the waitstaff came to the tables to serve different kinds of meat. We sat at our table and began to eat. The food kept coming, and there were different people entering and going out of the room as the options for food came through.

To set up the training, I had hired an individual to dress in dark clothes and enter the room. They would come in quietly and steal a purse. My objective was to have the team members describe what time the thief came in, what happened, and what they looked like. I knew that this exercise was important, and that it would provide key teachings that the staff could apply to their lives and careers. Often, it's the attention to detail that makes a difference. It's the small intangibles, the ones that most people don't see, that can be used to resolve a case or find a solution to an issue.

I didn't tell the team members who were training about the individual who would come in. Instead, I simply indicated they should know that the training would be going on during the meal. So, when an individual in dark clothing entered the room and grabbed a purse, I sat back to see who would react and how.

Notably, the one who acted first was a timid, quiet team member who doesn't usually speak up. She typically takes longer to share her opinion and always wants to be very sure of what she's going to say before she opens her mouth. As a rule, she listens before she acts.

That day, however, she spotted the hired purse thief. She saw the man take the bag, which belonged to a different team member, and move away from the table. She was sitting across from where this took place. In a quick movement, she jumped over the table, ran after the man, and caught him at the door. She grabbed him and said, "That's not yours."

One of the most intriguing parts of this training session was that she acted outside of her character. She moved impulsively in the setting. In doing so, she put herself at risk, and she could have caused a larger stir if the thief had been for real and had carried an armed weapon or had a history of violence.

Later, when we had a conversation with the team about the dinner and what happened, I told the woman who had leaped for the bag and chased the thief that she had done well to pay attention to detail. She watched her surroundings and noticed when some things were off. She chose to act based on what she witnessed.

After pointing out the positives, I mentioned areas where she could learn, stating, "You never run after a guy, as you don't know who he's with—there might be other people waiting outside. Certainly not for a purse that's not even yours." As part of the training, I covered some tactics that she could try in the future, and that the others could remember, too. "To start, you want to know how you would react in a crisis," I explained. "It's important to know how it feels, and what your intuition says. Once you're aware of that, you can choose to remain calm and do what you have to do next. To prepare, you'll want to know what your limits are, what your stressors are, and what your reactions are like."

To be a good leader in a crisis, you want to be decisive and not impulsive. There's a fine line between the two. You may need to take action, but you also have to have a scale. You need to know if you're willing to risk your life for another person. You want to think through what would cause you to run, and why you would stay in a place. You will need to know how you'll respond to questions you might be asked, and what you would do in a setting where you were injured or incapacitated. You must think through all these ahead of time. That way, you have a plan to follow if a crisis does occur.

In the case of the training session with the staged robbery, the takeaways included that the team member who reacted suddenly could have instead taken another moment to observe. She could have noticed what the man was wearing, what he took, and where he went. This way, she could have reported the incident later to those in authority. She also would have avoided the risk of putting herself in potential danger. If there had been others outside the door to the room, or a criminal who tended to be violent, the situation could have turned out to be very dangerous for her and potentially others.

BE READY TO ACT

Once when my kids were younger, we took a trip from San Francisco up to the mountains in Tahoe. We arrived in the Sacramento area along the way at about dusk and decided to make a stop at a gas station to go to the bathroom.

My daughter Vicki and I got out of the car to head inside. My husband stayed in the vehicle with the dogs and the youngest child, who was a baby at the time and was asleep. We walked across the parking lot to a building to find the bathroom, which was located around the corner of the structure, out of sight from our car.

We came out several minutes later and started heading back to our vehicle. All of a sudden, a man appeared and started following us. I immediately noticed and became very aware of his steps. I didn't know his reasons for following us, but I sensed something was off.

I recall what happened next so vividly that I can still see it in my mind. Vicki looked at me. I looked back at her. We both immediately knew what to do next. She was aware that I was going to get myself between her and the man following us, and that she would run back to my husband. We didn't exchange a word.

Instead, I turned around toward the man following us. I put myself between my daughter and the suspect. She ran to the vehicle and got inside. I stayed where I was.

The man ran off.

Obviously, he saw that the women he was after were alert, ready, and not easily surprised. We knew exactly what to do and when to do it. She was ready to take action and trusted me to do the same. I also got back in the car, and we continued our trip toward Tahoe.

This incident ended as it did because I had already prepared my daughter. We had already had the conversation about what to do when being threatened many times. We depended on each other, and we were aligned.

Making sure everyone knows what to do and when to do it is a sign of true leadership. You can train and prepare your team for the unexpected. You can have conversations and build trust with them. That way, when and if something does occur, you'll be able to move with confidence.

If you ask my daughter, she recalls many times during her growing years when I would ask her to notice the details of a situation. I might want to know the numbers on the car plates around us. Or I might ask the kids to tell me the color of the vehicle that just passed us. I would ask her and the other kids to collectively decipher a loud noise. Was it a gunshot? Was it fireworks? And so on.

She grew so used to answering my questions that one time when we were in Argentina, she noticed another vehicle was following us. "I win," she told me. I didn't know what she was talking about. She said, "You're having a car follow us, so that you could ask us about it. I already spotted it."

The only thing was … I hadn't set it up. So, my next steps included following a plan I had created for defensive driving. We got away and were safe in the end, but the incident is still etched in my mind and my daughter's mind. It was a sign of her training, which started early on and taught her to always be alert—and ready to act.

INTUITION MAY NOT FOLLOW THE RULES

When we teach our kids, we often instruct them to follow cultural norms and traditions. While this can be helpful, it's also important to let children listen to their own intuition. Sometimes, how they act might be contrary to what we are generally taught in society.

For instance, we might train our children to greet everyone they meet. If we go to a family gathering, they will be expected to say "hi" to everyone. Maybe we have a get-together with aunts, uncles, grandparents, and cousins. We could ask our child to give everyone a hug to say "hello."

What happens, then, if the kid doesn't want to give a hug to someone? Maybe they say, "I don't feel comfortable doing this. I don't care if he's my uncle."

We need to be respectful of the child's feelings in this situation. We have to give them an opportunity to say, "I don't like this." In the case of the uncle, if a child doesn't want to be around that relative, we will want to respect their opinion. We shouldn't push them to give hugs or spend time alone with a person who makes them feel uncomfortable.

The same is true in other cases. If your child is on an elevator, for instance, someone else might get on and join the crowd. The kid could sense something isn't right and want to get off. I always respect that and say, "Good for you. Get off." They may have just saved themselves from an unpleasant situation.

MAKE AN IMPACT

Whenever I give advice for corporate America, I share that it's so important to be yourself. The more you are you, the more people will respect that. They will appreciate your transparency and honesty. And when you are comfortable being yourself, you'll be able to better spot ways that you could make a difference. You'll need a careful eye and the ability to make decisions with the information you have on hand.

Earlier on in my career, I went to Peru to choose an outside counsel to represent an American company in the country. I was to choose a law firm that would serve as our outside counsel for a matter in that country. There was an organization in Peru that the firm had traditionally used for this. So, I started there as my first stop on the trip.

In preparation for the meeting, I saw that the files indicated all the outside counsel members at that time were men. I figured that we needed more women at the table. The company I was working for needed diversity, and people who could bring in different opinions and perspectives.

On the day of the meeting, I went inside the office to meet with the counsel members and make selections for the new team. I wore a pants suit that day, complete with a white shirt and blazer. When I arrived at the main conference room, I was greeted by men sitting around the table. All of them were older than me. Standing around them were women in nice jackets and skirts. The women's clothing all matched.

I started by asking the group who would be part of the working team for the company. They shared a list of names, and they were all men.

I looked at them and said, "What about any women?"

They didn't know how to respond, so I continued, "And why are all these women here wearing the same outfit? Because it caught my attention that everybody is in the same suit. Just the women are matching—not the men."

One of the leaders replied, "Well, we provide the suit ..."

Seeing the surprise in my face at this, he added, "Since women with pants are unacceptable."

I was taken aback. I said, "Well, I have two problems with that. First, either you don't realize that I'm wearing a pants suit, or you decided that you were going to offend me. Second, if you have only men on the working team, this means you don't have the best talent at the table. So, I'm not going to do business with you."

True to my word, we stopped using them and hired a new outside counsel firm.

While I felt my decision had been a good one, I also knew that I had spotted the nuances and stayed calm. I had seen that the women were all dressed the same, that they weren't in positions of leadership, and that the current counsel members weren't giving the women a voice at the table. I had to make a choice on whether to continue with them or do something else.

By the way, the women who were in that room and heard the conversation were so happy. Nobody before had ever called out their status in that way and spoken up for them. Years later, when our paths crossed again, they followed me around and continued to thank me.

Following that dismissal, I looked for another law firm. I picked one that seemed much more diverse and progressive. I contacted the partner at the place and set up a meeting.

When we were face-to-face, I told him, "We need new lawyers. We need women at that table. We need to break every single mold that keeps women at a disadvantage. I want the best of the best, no matter what color, what religion, or what gender."

"That's us," he replied.

As a test, I said, "Okay, we'll go with you. And now to celebrate, I want to go to lunch." I added that I wanted to attend a club nearby that was a place where only men were members.

He looked at me for a second. Then, he said, "You know it's only men."

"I know," I replied. "That's why I want to go."

So, he said, "Let's fix that." And he took me to lunch at the club, which traditionally had only male guests. That is, until my meal there.

That firm turned out to be as good as the partner had claimed. They had amazing women at the table and great men, too. We stayed with them for years.

OTHERS WATCH YOUR ACTIONS

When you notice the signs and act, people notice. And even if you don't see a reaction from them immediately, it's possible they'll file it in their minds. Later, they could act in a similar way based on the example you've set.

I remember going to a supermarket with my kids when they were younger, and it had a café inside. We stopped to get a snack on our way to an event and walked into the café to place an order. There were some little tables inside, along with a counter where you would order and pay.

As soon as we entered, I noticed there was a homeless man holding a cup. He was standing at the counter, trying to get the attention of the person behind the cash register. He held a $5 bill in his hand, which he waved to show he could pay.

Still, the person ignored him and kept serving the other customers.

I could tell that what was going on wasn't right. I watched a bit and noticed the other clientele kept getting served, while the homeless man was passed by.

When the cashier signaled that it was my turn, I went up to the counter and said, "Excuse me. This gentleman was ahead of me."

In response she said, "Oh, we don't serve people like that here."

"What?!" I asked. "Then I need to talk to your manager."

The manager joined the scene and explained, "Well, you know we have guidelines for this."

"Then, this man is my guest," I said. "And we're going to have a coffee."

I looked at the menu items and continued to order juices and food for us all. Then, I pointed to a place to sit down and said, "We're going to be at this table, and please serve us."

The homeless man sat down next to us, and I could tell he was uncomfortable. I told him, "You're my guest. You have nothing to be uncomfortable about. They're in the wrong, and we're here doing the right thing."

Then, I told the manager, "I'll be writing a letter about this, and trust me, I don't know what your guidelines are, but this is not going to make you look good."

Shortly after finishing the meal, the homeless man left. My kids didn't say much about the encounter at the café with the homeless man, but they saw what I did. They observed me noticing the signs and choosing my actions.

About ten years later, my daughter came up to me one day. By this time, she had a credit card of her own that was attached to mine. She often went out with friends, and I always checked the charges. She was a vegetarian at that time and went to places that served the food she liked.

"Mom, you're going to see a charge on the credit card," she began. "It's for burgers at McDonald's, which I don't usually eat as you know. But I was there, and they were not serving a man, and I decided to buy him lunch." She still remembered that time we bought a meal for a homeless man, and she was moved to help someone else in need.

If you pay attention to details, others will watch your example and follow your lead. If you're in a position of authority, it's important to have conversations about being aware with your team. When you're going into an investigation, you need to be ready to look for small things that could impact the outcome. No violent crime happens unannounced. Most things have signs that precede them, and it's up to you to find them.

And when you do, you could make a big difference—for yourself, for your kids, and for others who admire your leadership and follow it.

KEY TAKEAWAYS

- Creating routines and being attentive to details can help you detect and address unexpected incidents.
- Train yourself to notice subtle changes in your environment. You'll be able to quickly identify potential threats or unusual behavior.
- Be yourself and look for ways that your unique traits can be used to make a difference. You could inspire others to make changes in their lives too.
- As a leader, your actions, especially during a crisis, can influence how others react. If you're willing to stand up for what's right, others may follow and do the same.

CHAPTER 6

THE DIFFERENT SHADES OF GRAY

Some situations are clearly black and white. At these times, it can be easy to see what course of action to take. For the rest, you need to learn to navigate the gray. This refers to the many uncertainties we face when the answers aren't immediately obvious.

In January 2020, I was with my family in Hong Kong. We were spending some time there to enjoy the sights and meet up with friends. On one of our days there, I took the kids to the Disneyland Park in the area. My husband wasn't feeling well and stayed at the hotel.

When we returned from our outing, he shared that he had been watching TV and looking up information. "Have you heard of COVID?" he asked me.

"No," I answered.

"This is serious," he said. "We should go back to the US before we cannot travel anymore."

I could tell his intuition was guiding his judgment. I agreed, and we changed our tickets to an earlier flight.

Back home, when I went in to work, we started hearing about COVID-19 more and more. Still, nobody knew exactly what to do for the next couple of months. As more information became available, it grew clear that we were entering a crisis. I watched some leaders rise to the occasion and become stronger, more capable, and more confident. They communicated even better than before and had the ability to make decisions. Others froze and left their employees in a position where they didn't know what was expected of them.

At my workplace, I took a role of leading the efforts for communication about COVID-19. I spoke with the medical team and worked very closely with our HR department as we contemplated what to do. After rounds of discussions, we decided to take two weeks off. Before I left work to start the two-week period of remote work, I questioned whether to bring my computer as I had an iPad to use at home. In the end, I decided to keep the computer with me in case I needed a file from it.

Thankfully, I took it! Because we didn't go back to the office for the following two years. When I eventually returned, I found peanuts and goodies in my desk that had to be thrown out because they were so long expired. They were a clear reminder that nobody had left the office thinking they would be away for so long!

During those two years, there were so many changes to the way business is done. Doctors began treating patients online as a normal practice. Workers logged in from home and sat in on more video meetings. Companies watched their facilities' needs drop and office space vacated. For the C-suite, there was no longer a corner office, complete with a specially selected table, chairs, greenery, and artwork to mark your status. Instead, executives sat at home and answered their own phone. For me, I became the queen of my home office ... but it came with its own system. I can ring any bell I want, and I can also guarantee nobody will come running to see if I want coffee. The cocktail parties, summer picnics, and office lunches all disappeared, too.

As leaders, we had to think about how to engage people as well as retain workers. In the past, a company might hold in-person events for workers or give them merchandise, but those methods were either no longer options or were not as effective anymore. After all, who wants to wear a company T-shirt while they are working at home? They might opt for their own comfortable attire instead. Intentional communication was needed to stay in touch with team members and manage projects.

Month after month, COVID-19 presented gray areas where choices had to be made. We had to learn to live with uncertainty and make decisions. Would you send kids back to school and risk them getting sick? Would you stay home until they were fully vaccinated before going out? How long did you wait to travel again? How comfortable were you managing risk for you and your family?

While we may have moved on from some elements of COVID-19, the effects from the pandemic still play a role in our everyday lives. Macrotrends related to the way we live and work continue. We shop online more than ever, work from anywhere, and strive to maintain a balanced lifestyle.

The fact is, while portions of the crisis of COVID-19 may be behind us, another one will come at some point. Then, as before, we'll have to navigate the gray areas. This can include making decisions when it is not clear what is right and wrong, evaluating risk, and accepting the consequences of your decisions.

As you read through the following sections, think about your own values. Consider how they compare to others, and how they impact the risks you're willing to take. Also evaluate your approach to risk and recognize your options in every circumstance. When you do this, you'll be able to work through the gray, understand your risk tolerance, and be willing to look for the silver lining. Life will throw gray areas at you, and true leaders will rise to the occasion.

THE EFFECT OF NO VALUES

People who don't know what guides them may feel lost. They could make mistakes because they lack a set of values. They might be missing a sense of direction and not know their purpose. When this happens, it's easy to feel unfulfilled and to go astray.

In the corporate world, we often see negative effects when leaders don't carry a strong set of values. If your boss doesn't consider it important to have integrity, they might not treat others with respect. They could set a poor example for others in the workplace, too. If the leader isn't honest, why should the workers tell the truth? When the executive takes extra personal time, shouldn't others do the same, even if it's against policy?

An entire culture can be influenced by values. If team members are unaware of what role they play, they might be less inclined to accomplish tasks. On the other hand, when the leadership team acts with a purpose and sets a vision, it is often easier for the workforce to find their place and contribute.

In this way, people react the way they see others act. If their leader operates like a shining light in a sea of darkness, they could be inspired to be a light as well. They may work hard to implement a positive change at the company and support an upbeat culture.

This concept of values may seem gray, as it can be hard to immediately see what is important to a person. It might not come in the form of a written policy or report. Instead, we have to watch others to see what their values are. Once you know what is important to someone else, you can see if it aligns with your priorities. If it's a good match, you might work well together and inspire one other to continue living out their values. If your values are different, it's worthwhile knowing where you each stand. That way, you will each recognize what is important to the other person.

WHEN IT'S NOT BLACK AND WHITE

What color is an apple? When did the sun rise this morning? Which way is traffic moving? Is the rule outlined in our policies? For some things, the answers are black and white. In these cases, it can be easy to find what's right and wrong.

In most instances, however, the situations and the answers are far from black and white. We tend to operate in a world of gray. It can be hard to determine what the correct solution is. This is true in every industry, including the legal and compliance space, and in every aspect of life.

What happens if you break the law while trying to protect yourself? For instance, you might be in your vehicle, driving home from an event late at night. You might run a red light because your intuition kicks in as you feel someone suspicious may be following you.

In such a case, were your actions illegal? Should you get a fine or a ticket for running the red light? If so, was it still worthwhile doing to protect yourself? Personally, I can understand the need to make a decision for safety. I might say, "You just ran a red light because you were being followed? Good for you."

Or suppose there is a policy at your place of employment that states no funds will be given for hostage events. Perhaps you frequently take work trips to a country that has a high crime rate. What happens if you are on the road for business, and you get kidnapped? The kidnappers might demand a payment for your release and say they will kill you if they don't get the money. Should you tell them that there is a policy stating no funds will be transferred for your survival? What if your family pays the fee the kidnappers demand? What if a coworker sends company funds so you get released?

It can be hard to point to events like this one and claim the person was acting illegally. Perhaps they end up using company funds to free themselves or pay the ransom themselves and ask to be reimbursed. While this is breaking a policy, it is also a matter of survival. In such a case, I might say, "Congratulations, you just saved yourself. Now what I can also tell you is that the company cannot pay for it."

Nearly every situation has different shades of gray. We must account for the players, the time, and the location. In certain situations, there are specific behaviors that are allowed. And there are also some actions that could be considered unacceptable.

The tricky part of this is that we all have different values and different factors that motivate us. Some things might scare you but not your peer group and vice versa. For each of us, we need to identify the different shades of gray. Then, we can have honest and transparent discussions. We might say, "Let's move the dial a little bit to the white," or, "We're going to move the dial a little bit to the black." We might ask questions such as, "How are we going to navigate this? Are we okay with the consequences?"

When I was a girl, and the danger of being kidnapped was real, I thought that I would do anything to survive. I listed out the things I would be willing to go through if someone captured me. That way, if I did get kidnapped, I would already have a plan to follow. I had thought through my shades of gray and the choices I would make.

This is important because in every situation, once you make a decision, you'll have to live with what happens next. You'll want to make sure you're comfortable with the steps that are being taken. As a leader, you won't be able to ignore the situation or expect somebody else to make the decision for you. It's not realistic, because you'll have to bear the consequences of your decision (which could include the effects of not making a decision).

EVALUATING RISK

Several years, there was a serial killer who went after young women. After raping them, he would kill them. He was friendly looking, came across as confident, and seduced his victims.

This went on until he encountered a certain young woman who was different than his other victims. He first met up with her as she was carrying groceries. He came to her apartment building and insisted on helping to bring her groceries up the stairs. She refused at first, but he insisted, and eventually she relented.

When they got to the door to her unit, he wanted to come inside. Though she tried to refuse, he eventually entered her apartment. Then, he held a gun to her head and raped her. After that, he got up and went to the kitchen, turning up the music and closing the window on his way. At that point, she knew he was looking for knives and would be killing her next.

Upon this realization, she grabbed a set of sheets and came up behind him. She walked through her apartment and out the door, then went to the neighbor's apartment for refuge. She escaped the threat and survived.[10]

Her story shows that she listened to her intuition. She also understood the stakes. She could either be killed or try to attack

---

10 Gavin de Becker, *The Gift of Fear* (New York: Bloomsbury Publishing, 2000).

her predator. She might have been willing to do whatever it took to survive and took that risk.

Even if we're not facing a crisis for survival every day, there are still risks involved. It's important to know your values and use them to navigate gray areas. If you get upset, you'll get overwhelmed and won't be able to think clearly. So, keeping a clear mind, understanding your options, and knowing what's happening around you are vital in every situation in life.

PLAYING WITHIN THE LIMITS

I first met my good friend Hans Peter Hasler, who is managing director and owner of HPH Management, more than a decade ago. At the time, Hans Peter was the non-executive director on a board of the company I was involved with. I was focused on compliance and governance, and we soon established a strong working relationship.

As a senior executive and top-level advisor to the life-sciences industry, Hans Peter has managed the growth of leading pharmaceutical players and successfully launched several blockbuster drugs. While I learned many insights from Hans Peter, he also took note of my approach, which tends to be different and stands out.

The way I guide compliance is clear and unique, he told me. "Most of the lawyers I have met over the past thirty-five to forty years would rather throw stones in the way and make business difficult, instead of enabling it," he explained. "Saying no and not taking any risk is sometimes career friendlier. But progress needs some calculated risk."[11]

After meeting me, Hans Peter said his outlook on compliance changed. He now takes the same strategy that I advocate for, which

11 Hans Peter Hansler, Interview, January 17, 2024.

includes laying out the playing field. It involves listing possible actions or activities, then selecting what is worth doing and what will be avoided. Essentially, I opened his eyes to see how moves could be made with some risks, as long as the ball is kept in the playing field.

While it isn't always easy to lead in gray areas, it's also true that every crisis comes with a silver lining. If you can appreciate how the experience will make you stronger, you'll grow as a leader. When you choose to stay positive, you can influence your team to do the same.

For me, during the COVID-19 pandemic, I was able to eat meals at home every day with my family. The pandemic allowed me to work from my house and skip the commute. My family found ways to take short trips to the mountains and a nearby lake. We enjoyed barbecues outdoors. We really learned to enjoy life in a different way.

As I look back on that time, I can see how many lives were impacted by health conditions and disease. Certainly, there were medical hardships and risks to face. There was uncertainty about the future. We had to learn to be okay living in the gray and facing the unknown and still thrive.

In the end, I believe COVID-19, like many other crises, gave us the chance to choose how we would react. It was like a mirror in a way. You put it in front of your face, and it gives you the opportunity to really test who you are. We could be negative about the situation. Or we could be optimistic and look for ways to bring more light into the dark.

As you navigate the gray areas in your life and work going forward, remember that you can make a difference. You can choose to take on risks within the playing field. Making calculated decisions will help you demonstrate an attitude that looks to make moves and advance. When others see you do this, they may, like Hans Peter, join in and have a refreshing approach too.

KEY TAKEAWAYS

- Clear values are needed for leadership to give direction and set an example that others can learn from.
- Many situations present complex, gray areas where it can be hard to set a course of action. Leaders must navigate these settings by considering their values, motivations, and the impact of their decisions.
- Effective leadership includes balancing calculated risks while staying within certain guidelines. Leaders should encourage innovation and progress while following compliance and governance standards.
- Crises bring a chance for you to adapt and be resilient, and once they are past, you'll be stronger and more prepared for the next one.

CHAPTER 7

FINDING A NEW PATH

Years ago, I had a very difficult job. I found myself in a tough position, and every day was hard to get through. The work was not what I wanted, and I knew I couldn't continue in it.

Changing jobs, however, would not be easy. I was especially worried about how it might impact my family. We had just moved to a new state, bought a new home, and put our three kids in different schools. If I switched to a different job, we would likely have to move again. I didn't know that I wanted to put them through the change and upheaval.

I had to travel frequently for work at the time, and I remember a particular meeting in France that I attended. During the session, I saw the people I was working with for who they really were. I realized we didn't share values. By the time the meeting ended, I was convinced it was time to change and move on.

I was ready for a new path. For a better job. One that aligned with my values.

I just didn't know how.

As I sat on the plane flying from France back to the United States, I started writing out my plan. I knew I needed to get out of the situation I was in and find something else. The flight was a nighttime one, and I looked out of the window at the dark sky. As I thought about my job that I wanted to leave, I thought, "I cannot change the dark. I cannot change the day. But I can change how I react to all of this."

By the time the plane landed, I knew what I had to do. My plan was ready, and I would put it into action.

I remember getting back on the ground in the United States. I had to go directly from the airport to another work meeting. It was an important one, and I would have to make a stand during it. Specifically, since I didn't share the same values as the others I was working with, I knew I could be walking away from the meeting without a job. I essentially would be resigning without another position lined up or a two-week notice. I could lose my paycheck and our family's main source of income. Still, above all, I had to follow my values. If the decisions made at the meeting didn't line up with mine, I would have to leave. Staying wouldn't be true to myself.

On the way to the airport, I called my husband Clinton. The kids, our life, and our finances weighed on my mind. During that phase of our lives, Clinton had stepped back from his own career while I was pursuing mine. He had taken on many of the responsibilities for the kids and our home. I worried about what my decision might mean for the family, our life, and our well-being.

When Clinton picked up the phone, I said, "How much money do we have in the bank? I'm going into a meeting, and I might have to walk out."

Clinton, without missing a beat, responded, "Just do what you have to do. Do your professional best, baby. We will always be fine."

I resigned from the job that day.

To this day, I have no regrets. What happened in the days and months that followed ended up being what was best for our family and my work. We did move to a new place, where I took on a job that aligned with my values. I was well compensated for my expertise and leadership, and most importantly, I was where I wanted to be and who I wanted to be with. The kids, for their part, settled into new schools and routines.

Still, from this story, we can easily see just how hard it can be to change. We tend to be creatures of habit and crave consistency. Pushing into the unknown and a world of uncertainty is very difficult.

Yet, in reality, change is constant. Our loved ones grow, age, and move through different stages of life. The environment at our workplaces can shift, and the projects we oversee are all unique in some way. We might come to a point in our career when we want to do something else, or even pursue a different business idea. There's really no way to stop change from happening around us.

That's why we need to build our emotional intelligence and lean into our intuition. By being ready to face change, we can accept the fact that we feel uncomfortable. Even though it was not easy for me to step away from my job with no paycheck in sight from another place, it was worthwhile in the end. I knew I had drawn on my sense of duty to make a decision. As my husband Clinton mentioned, it's important to do what you need to do. When you put in your professional best and also account for your family, you'll come out ahead in the long run. In fact, you'll be even stronger.

In my case, I knew I was doing the right thing, and I had the courage to act. I freed myself up to pursue a path that would align with my values and give me a chance to make a difference for others. I ultimately moved up in my career, as I ended in a place that allowed me to create a positive impact for others.

In the following sections, I'll share ways that you can find a new path for your life and career. You'll need to surround yourself with people who want you to succeed and are willing to be with you in the good and the bad. You'll have to recognize your values and set up your schedule so that you can focus on your priorities. You'll want to be ready to make decisions when you realize that something isn't right for you. You'll also do well to remember that success is about more than just money, and I'll share my father's explanation about this concept and how it impacted me. Finally, know that when you're confident, ready to act, and willing to accept what comes as a result, you'll have the satisfaction of knowing you carried out your values to the fullest.

As you read through the examples and stories in the pages of this chapter, consider the decisions you've made in the past. Think about if you've leaned into changes, or if you tend to shy away from them. Look for areas in your life where there may be opportunities you could grasp. Even if it's uncomfortable at first, making a smart decision could lead you to a better place in life.

SURROUNDING YOURSELF WITH PEOPLE WHO WANT TO SEE YOU SUCCEED

My husband Clinton is a brilliant, well-accomplished person. He graduated from West Point and is highly educated and successful. When we got married, I felt I had put myself on a new path just by being around him. Throughout our time together, he has been dedicated and committed to making our relationship, and our family, work.

When our three children were young, Clinton and I recognized that we couldn't both have an intense, fast-paced, and demanding career without sacrificing our family. One of us would have to step back and support the other for a time. The kids needed someone who could take care of them and help them with the day-to-day routines. To keep our family strong, we wanted that person to be one of us.

As we looked at each of our careers, we saw that I had a meaningful opportunity at that time. Even as a young mother and executive, I was on a track to grow more. Given this, Clinton decided to support me in my career. He offered to take care of our kids and keep the family together.

Thus, he made sure the kids were ready for school, got home safely, and had their homework done. He made all the appointments they needed. He oversaw their art and music lessons and all their various activities during their growing years. He stayed home to maintain a consistent presence and helped them all learn the values of discipline he had been taught through his own military training.

As stable as Clinton was during those years, my job was the opposite. The hours varied, and I was often called in quickly to oversee cases. I traveled constantly and to places all over the world. The trips came up suddenly and on short notice—sometimes, I only had hours to pack before leaving.

One time, I was in a meeting, and my boss said to me, "Something happened in Belgium. Do you have your passport with you? You're leaving in two hours."

As I drove home to grab my passport, I called Clinton to tell him of the news. After I shared that I was heading to Belgium, I added, "I'm upset." I felt bad that I was leaving so quickly and wouldn't be around the family in the coming days.

"Save yourself from getting upset," replied Clinton. "It will make it more difficult. Everything's going to be fine. If going to Belgium is what you need to do to accomplish your mission, then go."

I went, as he said, and he was right. We got through the time away, and I returned home safely. Keeping a calm attitude and doing what had to be done helped us manage the situation and keep our family intact.

FOCUSING ON PRIORITIES: DO WHAT'S MOST IMPORTANT FIRST

Even as I carried an intense workload and maintained a schedule packed with meetings, I wanted to be involved in the kids' lives. I saw that I was a top earner and agreed with the decision Clinton and I had made to prioritize my career. I recognized that, as a female Latino executive who had children, I was in a very small minority group. There are very few examples of highly compensated executives who also have families. I could help to set an example for others to follow.

To perform well at both my job and at home, I realized I would need to prioritize. I wanted to communicate regularly with my kids. I also wanted to show up for my job and move up in my career.

When things are important to you, you become creative, and that's exactly what I did. I found ways to show love to my kids regardless of where I was. As a family, we worked hard to communicate often and clearly. Every night, I would call them before bed to "give them the dream" as we called it. I would ask, "What are you going to dream tonight?" The idea was that we would pick out something that was special to both the child and myself, then dream about it together. That way we could feel connected, even if we weren't in the same physical location. Sometimes, the dream would be about visiting my home country of Argentina together or about going to the beach. We might choose to dream of riding horses or to remember an experience that we had shared together previously. We also dreamed of the future and things we wanted to do later in life as a family. If I was on a plane or in a place where I couldn't call, I would write down the dream and send it to them.

I would typically call before school hours, too. It gave me a chance to say "good morning" to the kids and set the right tone for the day. I did this so often that they came to expect it. One time, while traveling in Switzerland for meetings, I was going to call my daughter Vicky before school. However, I missed the morning call in the United States due to the time difference and my commitments at work. So, I called a bit later, after school started.

When the receptionist at the school picked up the phone, I explained that I had missed talking to my daughter that morning. I mentioned I was calling to check in on her and asked if they could get her out of class so I could speak to her. When they did so, and Vicky came on the phone, I said, "It's Mom. Aren't you surprised that I called?"

"No, I was expecting your call," she replied. "It's late, but that's okay."

She was used to those consistent calls that she wasn't surprised! And really, those ongoing talks helped us get through both good and challenging times. If something happened while I was away, the kids could talk to me about it on the phone. You can have a strong presence even at a distance.

For important events, I always made sure I was home. When I was around, I would also take steps to help the kids manage their emotions while I was away. For instance, I used to mark my daughter Vicky's shirts. I would write "te amo" in the hem, which means "I love you." If she missed me while I was traveling, she could turn up the hem of her shirt and see those words. She now has a tattoo of those words in my handwriting on her wrist. This shows the strong bond and the reliance of our love since she was little.

MORE THAN THE MONEY

So often the idea of moving up is associated with monetary compensation, such as earning a higher income or getting a larger bonus. While compensation has a role in our lives, and I discussed earlier how it helped Clinton and I to make a decision about how to balance our careers, it isn't everything. I want to broaden the scope of the concept of finding a new path and point out that making a difference can be ultimately fulfilling.

My father used to say, "Anything you can buy with money is cheap." He was referring to other areas of our life that don't have a dollar sign attached to them. Money can't buy you a strong relationship with your family, it can't ensure you have a loving home, and it can't guarantee that you will feel fulfilled and like you are making a difference at work. These intangibles are often what bring us the most happiness in life.

I like to add to my father's phrase that, "If your only worth is tied to money, you're limiting yourself." Keep this in mind as you consider your life, your friends, your work, and your education. There are so many ways that you can learn and grow. You might look for ways to be a positive influence through your role at work. You could take classes on leadership or sign up for training to grow in confidence.

As you move forward, remember that our careers and personal lives are not a straight line. You might be doing something that you feel is important, and it may be worthwhile—even if you're not compensated for it right away. Over time and as you gain experience, you could find ways to move up and increase your salary.

In my case, I have often raised my hand and taken on an assignment if I felt it could be an opportunity to learn. I can remember when the OIG guidance first came out. OIG stands for the Office of Inspector General of the US Department of Health and Human Services. The OIG is responsible for combating fraud, waste, and abuse in health and human services programs, including Medicare and Medicaid. OIG compliance is legally required for healthcare providers and organizations.[12] When the guidance was first released, very little was known about it. My boss at the time asked a group of employees, including me, if anyone was interested in learning about it more and summarizing the information for everyone else. I raised my hand and said, "Me." I had no idea what compliance was at that moment. But I went to work and studied the OIG guidance carefully. I soon became the expert with OIG. And once I was the go-to person for it, a higher level of compensation followed. That said, I found it worthwhile to take advantage of the opportunity on a personal level too. It was a way to get on a new path and become more valuable to the company. I was simultaneously growing in my own knowledge and finding ways to help people even more. I could take what I learned and use it to guide decisions and stand up for what I believed was right.

Being involved in humanitarian aid and choosing to lead in a way that shows others you're interested in them rings true for my good friend Randy Bagwell, senior division director of the Asian Pacific Division and IHL (international humanitarian law) senior policy advisor at the American Red Cross. Prior to joining the American Red Cross, Randy served in the military, carrying out roles including an international law attorney and general counsel to Joint Base Lewis-McChord in Washington. When he left the military, he had numerous options he could pursue. He chose the nonprofit because, as he recalls,

---

12 "What Is OIG Compliance?" Verisys, January 8, 2024, https://verisys.com/what-is-oig-compliance/#:~:text=OIG%20compliance%20refers%20to%20adherence,programs%2C%20including%20Medicare%20and%20Medicaid.

"I wanted to do something that made a difference that was larger than what I do."[13]

This drive to help others started during his time in the military. Randy noted, "When I look back at what I accomplished in the military, the biggest one is not something I did back then, but rather what happened five years after I left. People that had been under me, and individuals I had mentored, grew to be the leaders of today. I know I had a part in shaping how they got there and building them up—that's really my legacy."[14]

Randy also sees parallels between his work and mine, as I also have always wanted to contribute in a way that mattered. In my role in compliance, I have helped pharmaceutical companies follow regulations and stay on track so that they can serve the public in an ethical way. It's a meaningful job, and one I take to heart. Making a difference can be more fulfilling than chasing a higher paycheck.

LIVING OUT YOUR VALUES

As concerned as I was about switching jobs when I was in an environment that didn't align with my values and needed to leave, I found that the eventual outcome was an overall win. I was given a very good offer for a job in California, and the company was willing to relocate my family and myself there. It wasn't the highest paying position that was available to me, but I knew that the CEO was an equitable person and that he was giving me the best he could. Since the company had similar values to my own, I knew it would be a better fit and worthwhile in the long run.

---

13   Randy Bagwell, Interview, 2024.

14   Ibid.

After moving out to California and settling there, I worked for the company for a full year. After contributing and working hard to make a difference, I brought up the topic of compensation. Even though money isn't everything, and is just one measure, I felt it was time to revisit the salary package. I was given a much more favorable offer that time around, including better benefits.

For my family's part, they ended up enjoying California, too. In fact, we now call it home. The kids found educational paths and career direction here. They even came to appreciate the many moves that our family took during my years of job changes and before we settled in California.

One routine I developed to live out my values involved taking my kids to Argentina during their summer breaks. While we were there, they would attend school as a learning experience. I always thought it was important that they honor my legacy and culture and their ancestors.

To be able to attend school in Argentina during the summer breaks in the United States, there was an admissions process to follow. Part of this included an essay in Spanish, and one year, my oldest son Maximo wrote out one as best as he could. He was a freshman in high school at the time. We sent the essay in and then waited to see if he would be accepted. We went to Argentina to visit family and be ready for the schooling there to begin.

Not long after sending in the essay, I got a call from the school principal. "We need to show you this essay. Can you come in?" He asked. When I arrived at the school, I saw that Maximo had written three pages. What had surprised the team members at the school was what he said about change. He had moved thirteen times by then. In his essay, he noted, "We moved a lot for my mom's job, and we had to change cities and friends and schools. We've been exposed to different cultures, and it has always made me better. It made me learn more about myself and how to relate to others." I knew I had made it as a mother when I could see examples like this. Maximo was understanding the strengths that come with change and adapting.

That summer in Argentina, at the school that accepted him and admired his essay, Maximo was very successful. He wanted to be a rapper and found out the school was having a talent show. A group of kids formed a band and asked Maximo to be the lead singer. His confidence and ability to adapt to change made him the perfect fit, and he embraced his role. At the talent show, his band performed the closing act. I attended the event and listened in my seat when they announced that "Max the rapper from the US" would do a song. I looked around the room and noted an audience of about two hundred people, many of whom were kids. Maximo came out and was greeted with hysterical applause. It was like a star had just appeared before us all. I looked at Maximo standing on stage and thought he looked like he was on top of the world. He delivered his song spectacularly and it was well received.

For Clinton's part, while he committed time to the family so I could focus on my career, he also found ways to take on some work opportunities that he could manage in addition to overseeing the kids. He carried out consulting projects, taught, and also accepted smaller roles. After the kids were grown, he dedicated more time to his own career. He became CEO of a company, did what he wanted to do professionally, and accomplished his career goals. Through it all, he kept the family and our well-being as his top priorities. The kids will often tell me, "I want a spouse who loves me as much as Dad loves you."

As you think about ways to get on a new path in your own life and career, I encourage you to think big and to be open to possibilities. Make sure that you're in a great place to start. If you don't get along with your coworkers, the culture isn't right, or the responsibilities don't fit with your strengths, it may be time to change. If you delay a decision, you're really putting your growth on hold. For this reason, you'll need to have high self-esteem, be ready to make decisions, and be willing to accept the consequences that follow, knowing that you're carrying out your values to the fullest.

When you look at salaries and ways to increase income, remember that success can come in various forms. I've been given country club memberships, cars to drive, access to boxes in sports centers, and more. You might be able to get significant benefits if you're open to possibilities that come outside of the paycheck.

A new path could even be related to the way you want to work. If you're currently going to an office every day, and would prefer to work from home, there could be a position that allows you to be remote. You might only have to go to the office a couple of times a week or not at all. If this is important to you, you may be willing to accept a lower level of compensation to get greater balance and a higher quality of life.

As you work toward your goals and upleveling, surround yourself with people who look out for you. They will support you and encourage you to make changes at the right time. They can be your sounding board, and the people you celebrate with when you get those fabulous wins.

KEY TAKEAWAYS

- Balancing work and family requires setting aside time to maintain relationships and keep the lines of communication open.
- Helping others and working to make a difference can be very meaningful in your personal and professional lives.
- When given the chance to try something new, be ready to step in. It could lead to the more doors opening for you at a later point and establish you as an expert.
- Surround yourself with the right people, who will support you through the challenges and celebrate the successes with you.

CHAPTER 8

SELECTING YOUR TRIBE

At one point in my career, when I was involved with a large pharmaceutical company, I learned of a kidnapping that had taken place. Two of the firm's US employees went to visit the general manager of the Latin American entity. While they were on the trip, a rebel group kidnapped them. The two employees were kept as hostages for more than a year while the kidnappers negotiated their release with the company. In the end, after eighteen long months, a payment was made, and the two employees were released.

The crisis affected many involved, from the families of the victims to the company they were associated with and the people working to help them return home safely. As I watched it unfold, it left a permanent impression on me, too. I thought about the two individuals during that intense time. They had traveled together from the United States to Latin America, where they were both kidnapped and held for ransom. Their experience showed that anyone you work with, or travel with, could potentially become a fellow hostage.

Given this, I began to reflect more on the importance of building a team you could rely on. There are risks everywhere, and crises do occur. If an unexpected event like a kidnapping occurs, you and the teammates you are with could suddenly be plunged into a fight for survival. Who would have the right mindset to get through it? Who would be able to lead the way to safety? Who could stay levelheaded and use emotional intelligence to navigate the crisis?

As I thought more about these questions and the idea of a team with a survival mindset, I also evaluated my own circumstances at the time. I remember looking around me and seeing my coworkers in a new way. I thought, "Would I want to be kidnaped with this person?" I knew that I personally had a survival mindset, largely based on my upbringing in a place where life-and-death moments could occur on any day, and we always had to be vigilant. I learned early on how to have a plan and use emotional intelligence to identify threats and resolve conflicts. When the two employees from the United States were kidnapped in Latin America, it caused me to broaden that perspective and realize that more people, including those outside of your immediate family and friendship circle, could be at your side in a crisis.

At the time of the kidnapping, I remember thinking that if I were kidnapped, I could depend on my own instincts and follow a plan. As a leader, you need to let other people know that you're worth following. You have to not only think strategically but also convince others that your option is the best viable choice.

The whole event, from the two US employees being kidnapped in Latin America to being released after a year and a half of negotiations, helps us to reflect on leadership. As you grow in your own career and look to gain a promotion or greater responsibility, think about how you would manage a crisis. Would you have a plan? Would you know who to call? Would you know how you would exit? What would your family be told? The answers to these questions need to be thought through ahead of time—before a crisis occurs. If a kidnapping takes place, you won't have enough time to think of a plan and choose someone who could jump in and negotiate on your behalf. You won't be able to quickly find an exit strategy and contact your family so they know what to do. It all has to happen beforehand. You have to set aside the time to understand the risks and decide how you'll react if something unexpected happens.

When we speak of survival, keep in mind that it really is an attitude. If a person has a survival attitude, they can stay calm during a crisis. They are able to think strategically, and both follow orders and give orders. While these leadership characteristics are always important, they become even more critical during a time of uncertainty. A life-and-death event is not the time to experiment and try something new, or to be paralyzed with fear and indecisiveness because you don't have a plan.

To help you think about your own survival mindset and how to surround yourself with others who share the same attitude, I'll share examples and stories related to crises and crisis management in the following sections. We'll start by looking at a situation that reflects what not to do. Seeing the mistakes of others can be useful, as it will show you what can go wrong, and how to get away from an unexpected threat. We'll also look at how you can work with others to build up their crisis capabilities, and how they can, in turn, encourage you to uplevel your skill set, too. I'll close by sharing some key tips for survival that my dear friend Donna Kinsey and I developed together. Donna is a training and development instructor with more than twenty-five years of experience in law enforcement and was the first woman to ever attend the FBI National Academy in the history of her department. We not only taught each other how to survive in our careers—we found ways to train others and prepare them as well.

As you read the following sections, I invite you to use the time to evaluate your own approach to team building and crisis management. Ask yourself, as I did, "Who would I want to be kidnapped with?" If you don't already have a list, you can start forming one. And if you do have an idea of the people you could be held hostage with, evaluate if any changes or adjustments need to be made. You'll want people you can count on, and who will be ready to survive with you—and help others survive, too.

A BOTCHED KIDNAPPING

In my line of work, I've seen time and again how crises can play out in many ways. The outcome is often based on the amount of planning that was carried out before the event takes place. If one party is prepared and the other is not, the people who have a plan will typically be in a better position to negotiate and have a result that is in their favor.

To see this in action, consider the case of another US pharmaceutical company. This organization had its general manager located in a Latin American country to oversee the operations that were carried out there. When the Thanksgiving holiday arrived, the manager celebrated the occasion in their home in the foreign country.

During the festive meal, there was an interruption. Suddenly, armed individuals entered the house. They grabbed the general manager and took him away.

The company that the manager worked for had a plan in place which spelled out what to do in the event of a kidnapping. I was involved in the corporation at the time, and my coworkers and I knew the steps we would take. We were well prepared to do what's best and to execute the plan.

The kidnappers, on the other hand, had botched their plan. They had made a huge mistake. It turned out that they had read the map incorrectly and arrived at the wrong destination. They picked up the manager of the US pharmaceutical company, but he was not the person they wanted.

Had the kidnappers done their job correctly, they would have double-checked the address. They might have had better surveillance and carried out more thorough research. They might have also known the size of the guy they were looking for. The general manager was much larger than the person they wanted to kidnap and didn't speak Spanish very well unlike the intended target.

This story teaches us an important lesson about preparation and crisis management. In a rapidly changing situation, unless you have the right leadership, the wrong things can happen. In the case of the kidnappers, they captured the wrong person, and when they realized their mistake, they let him go. As they were freeing him, they told him they were after someone else, which was another mistake on their part. The general manager could inform others what had happened, and with his help, we quickly told the individual who the kidnappers were targeting about the threat. He and his family immediately left the country and went to a safe place. In the end, the kidnappers lost completely, as they were unprepared and poorly led.

A TEAM OF WARRIORS

You can have a group of people go through the same set of circumstances and have different results. During a crisis, it often plays out that some survive—and others don't. Certain individuals will have a strong desire to make a difference, and they will tend to show others how to get through a difficult situation. In fact, in my experience, I have found that the leaders who are most successful are often driven to contribute and make a positive impact in the world around them. They are passionate about their role and naturally want to help others around them.

To make the biggest difference possible, and to be able to navigate crises in the best way, these leaders need a team with a survival mindset. As I mentioned, after the two US employees were kidnapped in Latin America and held as hostages, I started applying what I learned from that event to team building. When the *Guardian* interviewed me for an article on leadership, the reporter asked me to share the strategies I used to build my team. I shared with the publication and its audience my way of assessing people. I mentioned that I always looked for individuals who I would want to be kidnapped with. I added, "I know within two minutes of meeting someone whether or not I'd want to be kidnapped with them."[15]

I'm able to quickly evaluate and make a decision because I rely on my intuition. It tells me if the person I'm interviewing or sitting with has the capabilities needed to handle a crisis. I can easily determine if they are strategic, able to plan and execute, and adapt as needed.

As you build a team ready for a crisis, keep in mind that the numbers don't have to be large. In my life and work, I have identified a handful of people who can think strategically, have a survival mindset, and would have my back. I trust them and know that they trust me as well. They can think clearly when events are quickly unfolding, and they have high levels of emotional intelligence. Importantly, they carry themselves with integrity, are loyal, and have the courage to do what needs to be done.

---

15   Patricia Fletcher, "Know Who You Want to Be Kidnapped with and for More Tips for Leaders," *Guardian*, May 12, 2015, https://www.theguardian.com/women-in-leadership/2015/may/12/know-who-you-want-to-be-kidnapped-with-and-four-more-tips-for-leaders.

As my longtime friend and coworker Lucia M. Carrero-Rivera shares, "Fabiana develops teams, bringing out everyone's best qualities, always leaving opportunities to grow and always with a mindset for success. Her value and expectations are high not only for herself but for her teams. You will find that Fabiana's truth will always flow through."

Forming this type of team is critical to long-term success in both your personal and professional life, mostly because we will all face crises. From kidnappings to threats and natural disasters, unexpected events do occur, no matter where you are. Given this, we want to think about how we will respond, and if we will use the situation to come out stronger, wiser, and a better leader, or if we will let the event defeat us.

I was recently at a beautiful outdoor restaurant at a mall near my home with my team (the team that I would be willing to be kidnapped with!). While we were eating, we saw a crime scene play out. Two girls in the area were arrested for stealing cosmetics. The police who led the girls away drew in a crowd of onlookers. I knew, based on my experience, that the situation could easily escalate. So did my team members. Whenever there is a large group of people, you want to know where the exits are, what your plan is, and how you'll react. This way, you'll be better prepared if an emergency takes place. You also want to know how the people you are with will act. As it turned out, the scene came to a quiet ending. Had it gone another way, we would have managed it together.

Having a team with a survival mindset can do more than just increase your own chances of living through a crisis. It can help you stay calm and trust that you are with other competent individuals who will be able to contribute. They can help you come up with possible solutions, look for exits to use if needed, and be ready to negotiate.

SET AN EXAMPLE

Once you have others on your team with the right attitude, remember that training is an ongoing process. When you're in a leadership position, people will look to see what you do and how you carry yourself. Your choice of words and actions, along with how you handle challenges, could have a lasting effect on them. The team will look to emulate both your attitude and your choices.

To maintain a strong team, both at work and at home, take a look at these guidelines that you can put to use in your everyday life. By following them, you can demonstrate to others how they, too, can be at their best during changing times:

- *Trust your instincts.* As I've mentioned before, listen carefully to your senses and be aware of what they are telling you. Use your intuition as a guide, rather than any critical voices or negative thoughts in your head.
- *Competence over confidence.* Hard decisions, especially those made during a time of crisis, are hardly ever clear cut. Think about what you want to achieve. Draw on that goal and your reason for it. If you know you are taking action for the right reasons, you'll be more confident in the approach you take.
- *Look after yourself.* Even in a tense, fast-paced setting, take time to get physical and mental rest when you can. It will help you be a high performer and more alert when you're on duty.
- *Train to succeed and learn to fail.* Aim to win but don't ignore the fact that there could be lessons to learn along the way. Imagine what success will look like. To get through a crisis, what steps will you need to take? Once you're out of it, how

will you feel? Use this visionary exercise to motivate you to keep working toward the goal.[16]

BUILDING UP OTHERS

As I referenced earlier, my good friend Donna Kinsey and I have worked together to share information and training resources on having a survival mindset. While our discussions and workshops serve to mentor others, we've also applied these teachings to our own lives. In fact, when we first met, we used some of the techniques we now teach to our audiences on each other.

Donna and I became friends when two of our children attended the same elementary school. We were both involved at the school, and we hit it off right away. Donna was working in law enforcement at the time, though she was looking for a way to grow in her career. The only problem was, she couldn't find opportunities to do so.

Donna remembers reaching out to me for help in her professional career, too. She shares, "When we first met, I would ask, 'How did you get to where you are? What struggles did you have to face?' There was a level of confidence that I had never seen in another woman, and I had always strived to have that kind of confidence, too."[17]

By the time we met, Donna had been in police work for some time and had tried to move up, but over time had felt stagnant. "The higher up in rank I went with the police department, the more of a threat I became to the male-dominated field," Donna recalls. There were no other women in positions of leadership, and she eventually felt she could no longer get a promotion. It seemed it would rock the boat too much to have a woman in high leadership. "For years I was

16   Ibid.

17   Donna Kinsey, Interview, 2024.

assigned to the community policing section," Donna says. "Regardless of the rank I achieved—and I went from sergeant to lieutenant to commander and then major—they really wanted to keep me in community policing." She enjoyed the work but longed for something more. She wanted to try new things, take on different challenges, and learn and grow. She was looking for a way to survive as a woman trying to move up in a career where she was a minority.[18]

Eventually, Donna decided that her chances of getting a higher position in a different department were remote. "I pretty much gave up, and I gained a tremendous amount of weight," she shares.[19] She didn't have any other female mentors or role models at work, and no woman in her workplace was in a higher position either.

Then, suddenly, the department hired a new police chief. "As luck would have it, our city went outside of the department to promote a police chief, and they hired a female police chief. It really shook things up in the department," Donna recalls.[20]

Not long after that, the new police chief called Donna into her office. The chief brought up the FBI National Academy, which is a ten-week course for law enforcement executives at high-ranking levels that is held at the FBI headquarters on the Marine Corps base in Quantico, Virginia. It is often considered the premier law enforcement training on the planet and is highly competitive. Command-level officers usually wait years to get in once they throw their name into the hat.

So, when the police chief brought up the FBI National Academy, Donna listened. The chief started talking about other police officers in the department who had attended the training session. Then, the

18   Ibid.

19   Ibid.

20   Ibid.

chief asked why Donna had never gone. "I told her I knew I would never get the opportunity to go," she says.[21] Besides the fact that she had always been passed over as a woman, she also recognized that there were guidelines. To be eligible, there were height and weight requirements. Donna was about one hundred pounds overweight at the time.

Since it usually takes a couple of years after applying to be accepted, the police chief proposed a deal. She told Donna she would put her name in and requested that Donna lose weight to get ready. "I walked away from that meeting knowing that if I let that opportunity go, I would regret it for the rest of my life," Donna says.

That's when she turned to me again. She had asked me previously about moving up, as she had seen my career and track record as a Latina woman. She recognized I had survived, even though I was a minority, and had even broken through many barriers to achieve a higher position in my field. When Donna talked to me, she wondered how she would be able to hold her part of the deal and lose the weight.

I told her, "There is no way you are going to let this go. You're going to start working out. You'll get up in the morning and go running. You'll eat healthy and drop the weight."

During the next months, I kept calling Donna and encouraging her to lose the pounds. She followed an exercise routine and dropped about eighty pounds in twenty-nine months. It was a tremendous accomplishment and far from easy to achieve.

Around that time, the police chief called in Donna again to let her know that it looked like the doors were opening to her at the FBI National Academy. "I just said, 'No, I give up. It's not going to happen,'" recalls Donna. She didn't yet fit the weight requirements and feared she wouldn't be able to make it in time for the training.[22]

---

21   Ibid.

22   Ibid.

I proposed a new plan for her. I told her to build a portfolio, complete with 8 × 10 pictures of herself to document her progress. I explained she could show her "before" and "after" pictures to the staff members at the FBI field office in the area, which was sponsoring her entry. She could tell them how far she had come and her plans to drop the final pounds.

She followed my advice and prepared for the meeting. "I took this portfolio to the FBI field office and met with the staff members," Donna says. "Their jaws dropped when they saw the pictures. When I finished my presentation, they said, 'You're going.'"[23]

Shortly after, Donna attended the ten-week session at the FBI National Academy. "It was a life-changing experience for me," she says.[24] She trained with 250 other law enforcement executives from all over the world. When she returned, she got the change of position she had been wanting for so long. She was put in charge of the Firearms Training Center.

SHOOTING RANGE

Just as I had helped Donna gain confidence and grow in her survival mindset, which she could then use for the rest of her career, she also offered me assistance when I needed it. When we became friends, I was working in a position where I had security professionals reporting to me. I found there was a lack of respect in the department, and the reports I received from those I was supervising didn't always contain the information I requested.

One time, I corrected a report with red pen and sent it back to the security officer. The man was so upset that he came to my office,

---

23   Ibid.

24   Ibid.

holding the marked-up document in his hand. As he put it on my desk, I knew we were going to discuss it. He started by saying, "First of all, nobody has corrected a document like this since I was in grade school."

"Oh, you don't like red?" I replied casually. "What about green? What's your color? Because unless you write something that's acceptable to me, this is how it's going to be corrected."

Ignoring my comment, he went on to say, "Second, I don't report to a woman."

"Well, you do have a problem there," I replied. "Because at the end of the day, I am me, I am here, and that's not going to change. And I'm the one who decides whether you work here or not. So, I'd get on with the times."

He still wasn't ready to go. "Third, I don't report to somebody that doesn't know how to shoot," he said with a tone of finality.

Interestingly, at the time of our conversation I did know how to shoot. I chose to not say anything right away. Instead, I waited until the security officer left my office. Then, I formed a plan in my head and picked up the phone to call Donna.

"I need to be able to shoot center ten times in a row," I told her. I knew she was the firearms instructor and could help me uplevel my game. I was also aware that she's an amazing shooter herself.

She agreed at once and invited me to the range where we could practice. The day of our appointment, I showed up wearing my usual attire: a black business suit and heels. When Donna asked me if I wanted to change, I told her I was ready to go the way I was dressed.

We got our equipment ready, including our earmuffs and glasses, and went to our lane. It was crowded that day, and we were the only women at the range. We started shooting, and soon, the men in the lanes next to ours stopped what they were doing. They watched us shoot—and we kept hitting our targets, again and again.

After Donna gave me training, I felt I was ready to reveal my skills to the security officers I worked with. I called the team together and said, "Why don't we go shooting as an exercise?" Everyone readily agreed. Then, they started talking as if only the men were going. Toward the end of the discussion, I asked, "Do you mind if I go?"

They stopped in mid-conversation and looked at me. "Are you—?" They couldn't even finish the question about whether I was serious, or if I was actually someone who could shoot.

In the end, I went along. After we arrived at the shooting range, I put on the right equipment. And when it was my turn, I hit straight center and better than anyone else in the group. The men on the team turned to me with their mouths open. "Oh!" was all they could manage to say.

"Exactly. In your business you cannot assume anything," I replied.

I gained their respect that day. Our working relationship improved, and they saw that I not only knew how to shoot but I also knew how to lead a team. We could work together to get accurate reports and be prepared to handle whatever came our way.

DEVELOPING A SURVIVAL MINDSET

After I helped Donna build confidence and go to the training she had only dreamed of doing, she committed herself to helping others. As the years passed, I found myself calling her again and again. She often came to carry out trainings at the companies where I worked. She has taught personal safety and carried out security assessments. She started a consulting firm and teaches personal safety to civilians as well. Her company has even been contracted by Caliber Press, a gold standard law enforcement training company. One of the courses she teaches is called "Women in Command," and she is always looking to mentor other women. "If there's something that I learned from Fabiana, it's that we can open the doors to other women and encourage them to come up through the ranks," she says.[25]

In our work together, Donna and I created a list of the top survival mindset safety principles. They are directed especially toward women and aim to help you significantly reduce your chances of being a victim of a violent crime. Donna and I have identified, along with other security experts, that there are three elements to a crime: a victim, an offender, and the opportunity. The tips we created help to change behaviors, which can in turn eliminate the opportunity.

Try out these behaviors, which we first published in *Hispanic Executive*, to create a survival mindset:

1. *File a travel plan.* Tell someone where you are going and how you plan to get there. List the dates you'll leave and when you'll come back. If the police don't have an indication of where you are, the people with this information will know where to start looking.

2. *Value your life more than anyone else.* Don't rely on others, such as the police, to protect you. Officers will usually respond to a scene after a crime has taken place. Bodyguards, armored cars, and security officers all play a significant role. Still, nothing can protect you better than your instinct, preparation, and ability to be aware of your surroundings and notice when patterns change.

3. *Know the lay of the land.* Look at a map to see where you're going and follow your route. Notice landmarks and pay attention to your surroundings. If you see objects that stand

---

25   Ibid.

out, such as bridge or tall building, make a note. If you have to call for help, you'll be able to share details about your location.

When you're traveling to a different country, learn the language if possible. Also pay attention to cultural norms. Act appropriately and be cautious of anyone who does not follow the accepted practices. When arriving at an airport to be picked up, set up a way to meet with the person who will take you to your destination. Avoid signs that list your name and company, which anyone can see (or create). Choose a discreet method, such as having your pickup person hold a sign with a number rather than a name. Before you travel, get a picture of who will be meeting you, agree on the number, and you'll be able to find each other.

4. *If you think you are irresistible, think twice.* If someone suddenly acts as if they are infatuated with you or knows too much information about you, don't get involved. They may be targeting you or trying to convince you to go somewhere with them. They might also want to extract details from you about a person they want to capture or a project you are working on. I always advise reminding yourself, "Nobody is that good looking." If you see somebody twice, chances are that you're being followed. If something is out of place, pay attention to the warning signs.

5. *Trust your gut feeling.* As a recurring theme in this book, listen closely to your senses. If you feel danger is present, that could be a signal that you should get out of the area. Be ready to say "no" to a stranger who wants to come in, even if you can't quite give a logical reason to explain why. It could be your gut alerting you to something that is off, and by listening to your intuition, you could get safely inside, alone.

6. *Hit it and quit it.* Move toward your destination as if you are on a mission. Make direct eye contact with others around you and let them know you see them. Act confidently and avoid getting distracted when searching for your car keys or trying to remember where you parked.

7. *Trust no one.* Remember the phrase that children are often told, "Strangers are anyone that we don't know." If someone that you've never seen before comes to your home or hotel room door, you don't have to open up. Always look through the privacy hole to see who it is before you reach for the doorknob.

8. *The more the merrier.* If you're traveling, don't be quick to go out on the town by yourself. Rather than taking a walk in the neighborhood, stroll through the hotel. Work out in the fitness center where you're staying or do a workout inside your room. There's safety in numbers, and you'll want to avoid being the only jogger running through a park in the early morning hours. Keep a low profile and avoid making copious credit card charges or large cash withdrawals when you're out by yourself, as it could draw attention.

9. *Refuse to be a victim.* If an offender tries to get you into a vehicle to go to a different location, never get inside. Fight back, run in a different direction, or scream. Do whatever you can to get away and call attention to the scene so you can get help.

10. *Remember the three Hs. Hit hard, hit fast, and haul ass.* If you react in the first few seconds of an attack, you substantially increase your chances of escaping. Your offender will likely be expecting that you will go along with the plan. Instead, do the unexpected, and hit hard, hit fast, and haul ass. Once you break away, run and get some distance between yourself

and the attacker. It's very difficult to hit a moving target, so by running you could save your life.[26]

THE BENEFITS OF THE WARRIOR TRIBE

Not long ago, I went with my sister Valeria (who I would be kidnapped with!) on a cruise to Antarctica. During part of the voyage, we looked out at the frigid waters below us. The water was so cold that if you immersed yourself, hypothermia would quickly set in.

Having my sister with me was reassuring. I could trust that she wouldn't do anything that might upset our travel, and she would also watch out for me. If I had suggested we try getting close to the water, she would have stopped me in an instant. The risk was simply too high.

At one point of the cruise, my sister and I ran into a different traveler from the United States. She was looking for information about kayaking. Apparently, she was hoping to go for a ride over the deathly cold waters.

As we spoke with her, I asked, "Do you kayak?"

She was from Florida but had never been kayaking before.

I looked at her and said, "If you never kayaked when you were in Florida, why would you want to kayak in the middle of Antarctica?" I knew that one mistake could cost her life.

We could reflect on this situation and point out that the woman seemed to lack a strong warrior tribe with her. She didn't have anyone looking out for her (at least to my knowledge) who was traveling with her. While my sister and I mentioned the risks, we also realized that if she had a strong team with her, the option might have been taken off the table before she started asking others for help finding a kayak.

---

26 Fabiana Lacerca-Allen and Donna Kinsey, "White Paper: 10 Things That Can Save Your Life," *Hispanic Executive*, September 24, 2014, https://hispanicexecutive.com/self-defense-white-paper/.

In my case, I always surround myself with a group that I would be willing to be kidnapped with and that I would be willing to go through any crisis with. They would take measured risks, they would be courageous, they would be team players, and they would be willing to serve others. This applies to both my personal and professional life. I need others who will take precautions with me. I want companions who share my values and have the courage to do the right thing, even when it is difficult.

If you do the same, you'll reduce your risk of mishandling a crisis. You'll also increase your chances of staying safe. This could apply to kidnappings, violent crimes, and other unexpected events. Together, you'll be able to support each other, encourage one another, and be ready to face whatever crisis comes your way. And once you get through a tough situation, you'll be even more confident and prepared to handle the next.

KEY TAKEAWAYS

- Critical events give us an opportunity to learn and think about how we would want to react if we were in that situation.
- Having a survival mindset can help you reduce your chances of becoming a victim. You may also be able to help others who are at risk.
- When building your warrior tribe, look for others who share your values and would be ready to act with integrity in a crisis.
- Having a strong team in your personal and professional lives can give you the assurance that you'll be able to face challenges and move past them.

CHAPTER 9

SPEAKING YOUR MIND IN LEADERSHIP

In my line of work, I've seen that it can be easy to be a good leader. However, to be an exceptional leader, you'll want to present more than your skill set every day. It will be important to bring your values to the table. One of these values should be empathy, so that you can relate to others and show that you care about them. You'll also need passion and a drive to really help others. You'll want to be doing something that's a service to the community and provides an opportunity for you to give back.

I carried all these values on my shoulders when I first met my good friend Randy Bagwell. It was early on in my career, and I was selected to present at the annual Interamerican Bar Association Corporate Governance conference. I was the leader of the corporate governance section. The man who had mentored me and promoted me to help me reach that opportunity told me, "Fabiana, you have to tread carefully, because some people there won't want to hear this."

"Well, then you chose incorrectly because I'm going to be me," I responded.

I chose a subject to present on that was considered a very touchy matter. It dealt with the question, "How can you talk about ethical governments and ethical corporations when the people in one country are being killed due to the lack of security?" I could see that those two components—ethics and lack of security—didn't go together. There was a father whose son had recently been killed in Argentina after an attempted kidnapping, so I invited the father to speak.

When others heard of my plan, they advised me that it could ruffle a lot of feathers. One of the few supporters was Randy's boss, and he and I were on friendly terms. He was the president of the military law section, and he told me that he loved my courage. He went on to say, "I hear that you're giving a speech that's going to ruffle a lot of feathers. We'll be there to support you."

I ended up giving the presentation I had prepared and discussed the juxtaposition of ethical guidelines in countries where security wasn't present. It went well, and Randy and I spent a lot of time together, we became friends, and had great conversations about managing risk and crises. That was the beginning of a lifelong friendship.

Over the years that followed, we've remained in contact, and I often turn to Randy when I need a crisis expert. Through talking to him, coupled with my own experiences, I'm convinced that if you can manage a crisis successfully, others will follow, and you will make a difference. Others will feel a sense of comfort when they're around you.

As we've discussed throughout the book, there are ways to develop these leadership traits. Once you have them and are living out your values and looking to give back, there could be high-ranking positions that become available to you. In my case, this has come up in the form of serving on boards. I now mentor others who are looking to grow and contribute to a greater cause.

There is a strong need for more women and minorities on boards for public companies in every industry. Consider the following statistics to get a picture of public boards. Among Fortune 500 companies, Hispanic board members have just 4.7 percent of the seats, Asian and Pacific Islander board member have 5.4 percent of the seats, and African American/Black board members have 11.9 percent of the seats.[27]

It's a movement we can all get involved in, and I'll start the discussion my sharing some of my own experiences on boards. We'll also look at the benefits of being on a board, and how you can get started in this area too. As you consider how you want to lead, think of opportunities that might provide a way to give back in a significant way. What you do could impact not only this generation but the ones to come.

EARLY BOARD EXPERIENCE

Given my background in leadership, and how I had taken on great amounts of responsibility at an early age, it was a natural fit for me to join GLOW Red. This is the Global Network for Women Leaders in the Red Cross Red Crescent Movement, an international group for women leadership. It was created in 2018 in response to the need to ensure the Movement's commitment to address "gender equality and equal opportunities at all levels of their own leadership bodies."[28] I

---

27 "New Data from Deloitte and the Alliance for Board Diversity (ABD) Reveals Continued Focus Is Necessary for Fortune 500 Boards to Be More Representative of the US Population," Deloitte, June 15, 2023, https://www2.deloitte.com/us/en/pages/about-deloitte/articles/press-releases/new-data-reveals-opportunity-for-growth-on-fortune-500-boards-to-be-more-representative-of-the-us-population.html.

28 GLOW Red, "About Us," Glowred.org, https://www.glowred.org/about-us/.

was invited to participate in leadership training, and it gave me the opportunity to mentor many women from Latin America.

I remember one lady from Guatemala who attended the sessions I was giving. She came up to me and said, "I want to be as confident as you are."

I responded, "You can. Nothing is stopping you." Even as I spoke those words, I understood that she had been raised in a different way. She had not been taught to make a statement in the way that I had. I added, "It requires training." It was a good chance for me to help her get further instructions and develop her self-confidence.

Randy observed what I was doing and suggested that I try sharing advice in a more formal manner. I had enjoyed mentoring and agreed with his suggestion. I met Hanna Malak, the regional CEO at the American Red Cross in San Francisco.

I started serving as the chair of the Board Development and Engagement Committee for the organization. In my role there, I drew on the extensive network I've built up over the years and brought in other board members with diverse backgrounds. I worked with the board to follow agenda-driven meetings and to achieve goals that would make an impact for the community. When referencing me, Hanna shared, "Fabiana is that special combination of humanitarian, leader and team player; she's approached her role on our board of directors with gusto … she's an advocate for diversity within our board."[29]

PARTICIPATING IN PUBLICLY TRADED BOARDS

Though I was aware of the statistics related to board members and minorities, that didn't stop me from applying to positions where I

---

29   Hanna Malak, LinkedIn, August 31, 2023, https://www.linkedin.com/in/flacerca.

thought I could be useful. The first publicly traded board that I sat on was for a company called Arthrocare that was under an OIG investigation. It looked like they were going to end on a corporate integrity agreement (CIA). I had become an expert in CIAs and knew that I could help. The company was also looking for someone with my level of compliance knowledge.

So, I put my name out, and I also knew that executives at Arthrocare were interviewing other people. When it was my turn to be interviewed, I had to fly from Las Vegas, where our family was attending a wedding, to the appointed place. I remember Clinton telling me before I left, "Don't take it the wrong way if they don't choose you." He was recognizing that it was very hard to get in. There were no women, and certainly not any Latinas, on the board. "It's not because you're not amazing," he added. "But things like this happen."

I turned and looked at him and said, "If they're truly serious about wanting compliance experience, they're going to pick me."

Off I went, flying to the interview and showing them who I was. It was over quickly, and they chose me.

I loved the experience. As my first time on a publicly traded board, I came ready and prepared. I had read and studied everything that I needed to so that I could understand their situation. I saw that being on a board meant discussing strategy and corporate governance at the highest level. We would talk about what was going to happen next, and how it would happen. I was able to contribute in a meaningful way, due to my extensive background in compliance, leadership, and CIAs.

After some time, the company was acquired, and the board members had to resign. I looked for another board experience and found another position through my connection with Hans Peter Hasler of HPH Management. By then, I had built up my network and was always ready to give my time and answer questions to those who came to me. Some of the boards I became involved with included Shield Therapeutics, the Center for Excellence in Life, and First Tee of East Bay.

Even though my strength remains in pharmaceuticals because I worked for so many years in that industry, I have found that I can contribute to other sectors as well. I have the capabilities to serve on boards for various industries, as the technical skills required for each are often similar, the experience needed is the same, and the leadership traits are similar, too. Everything else can be learned. Importantly, there is risk in every industry. Having to evaluate and manage those risks is an ongoing exercise, and I can often help navigate companies through complex situations.

BECOMING BOARD READY

For those who are looking to take on a board position, I always start by emphasizing that you should manifest your intention. Prepare yourself for the role and be clear on what you can contribute. If others know what you bring to the table, they can see if your knowledge matches with their needs.

Building up relationships falls into place here, too. You'll need to have discussions with others, so they understand your capabilities and what makes you stand out among others. As you reach out, avoid simply asking for what you need. Offer yourself and your services. Be ready to help without asking for something in return or compensation. You'll create trust and start to be seen as an authentic leader.

As you're considering board positions, make a list of organizations that you feel you could help. Study them and learn about what they are going through. Then, look to see how you could make a difference for the organization by being a board member.

SPEAKING UP

Part of the development toward becoming a board member can include public speaking. I began teaching and sharing my experiences at a young age. I remember one of my first speeches very well. It occurred during a visit to Argentina. By then, I had my master's from UCLA and was living in the United States. However, I had taken some time to come and see my family.

While I was there, my father invited me to join him at a club he frequented. It was a place where most of the members were men. We knew that while we were there, we would hear others discuss the issues of the day, which included topics related to Argentina becoming a democracy.

When we arrived, my father received a warm greeting. Then, the other men at the club turned to me and said, "Fabiana, since you're here, why don't you share your opinion on what the youth can be doing to make a difference?"

My heart raced. I wasn't expecting to be asked to give a speech. Moreover, I didn't want to let my father down. I agreed and went to the front of the crowd. As soon as I started talking and sharing my experiences, it became very easy. I soon realized I was in my element. I knew what I was talking about. As I stepped down, amid a warm reception from the audience, I could tell it had been a success. My father was so proud of me.

I still give talks today. It's important to do, because many times you're making a difference in the lives of those listening. When you're talking about touchy subjects, you might resonate with someone in the crowd who is inspired to make positive decisions. They might find it easier to cope with a trauma they are facing or be motivated to advocate for themselves.

I remember one big technological conference where I presented. The audience consisted of female leaders, and I shared insight on how to overcome difficult times and become stronger. I told how hard experiences could be leveraged to be a better leader. When I finished and left the main area, there was a woman waiting for me. She told me that she had been raped and had never had the courage to say anything about it previously. After listening to me speak, she felt she could talk about it.

Then, she asked, "How would you go about it?"

I said, "First I would talk to my parents and husband. Once you do that, you will feel stronger on what to do next. It will come to you, and I'll be happy to help in any way I can. But I think the best thing you can do is go and talk to other victims who had similar situations."

These days, when I speak to an audience, I let them know that I have faced challenges, and been scared and doubtful, too. I've been in situations where I didn't want to be, and I've made mistakes and learned from them.

Letting others see your human side can make you more relatable. People will realize that you're not untouchable.

MAKING A DIFFERENCE

In every area of your life, keep in mind that there are many ways that you can help. Spending time individually with a person can be meaningful. Speaking to a group serves a purpose, as does investing time with your children. Serving on a board can be another part of giving back, once you've made the right connections, know who to contact, and can show how you'll contribute in a valuable way.

When you follow your passion, you'll be motivated to overcome challenges and improve the lives of others. "I wake up every day excited to do the work that I do," Hanna says. "I know I'm making a difference. I'm literally helping to save lives, and I'm just proud to do that work."[30]

You may also find ways to train up future leaders. "The two biggest things where we need to invest our time and our thought are on who to hire and who to promote," Randy says. "It matters because it involves who you're bringing on your team. And that's who's going to lead your team. We want to invest in them to be the next generation."[31]

Another key part of building up the next set of leaders involves taking the time to help them develop. "The way to look at it as a leader is to consider it part of your obligation to take care of the people you have," Randy says. "Even if they leave and go out to other organizations, they could become partners of ours down the road." For this reason, it's worth taking the time to ask them what they want to achieve, what success looks like for them, and to help them lay a path to get there. This way, even if they don't stay within your organization, you can remain on good terms.[32]

Throughout your career, you'll be able to find ways to give back—you just need to look for opportunities. Once you've gained leadership experience, you may decide, as I have, to dedicate time to boards. It's a place where you can help make decisions that could positively impact families, communities, regions, and even the world.

---

30   Hanna Malak, Interview, 2024.

31   Randy Bagwell, Interview, 2024.

32   Ibid.

KEY TAKEAWAYS

- Serving on a board can be a way to provide insight, share your expertise, and make a difference for many others.
- Leaders speak up in a way that aligns with their values, and they work to always maintain integrity.
- If you're passionate about a certain cause, you can find ways to volunteer your time or resources to make a positive impact.
- It's important to always look for ways to give back, both to others in your circles at home and at work and to the wider community, so you can help as many as possible.

CONCLUSION

When I was young and living in Argentina amid the military dictatorship, I became aware of how essential it was to have a plan. My father first instilled in me the need to be prepared. As a girl, I didn't know just how far the ability to plan would take me. Yet, as the years passed, I used that key strategy to move to a foreign country, get highly educated, take on leadership roles at a very early age, move up the corporate ladder quickly, and even find my husband and build a family that fill me with joy.

Today, as I look back on it all, I'm glad I went through what I did. You see, we have choices to make about our circumstances. We can resist change or embrace it. And we can use the challenges we face to become stronger, to build resilience, and to find solutions. I'm convinced that my background helped me become the strong warrior that I am today. When I show up, I come prepared, excited to make a difference, and always looking to lend a hand.

Through it all, I've been guided by my values. If a setting didn't align with my beliefs, I found a way to change and take a new course. I've surrounded myself with a team who would support me through the highs and be ready to be with me during the lows. I've developed ways to identify individuals I would want to be kidnapped with and brought them into my inner circle.

In critical moments, I have leaned into my intuition to guide me. I've drawn from a high self-esteem to make decisions and accept the consequences. I've grown in my emotional intelligence and used it to navigate high-stakes negotiations, which has often put me at an advantage. This calm approach gets me through both the good times and the challenging ones. As I like to say, "If I'm not getting shot at, it must be a good day."

After reading this book, I hope you will take some time to really dig into your values. What are your priorities? How can you live them? Who do you want to be with? What people will make you stronger and be ready to fight for survival next to you?

For me, the biggest compliment in my life has been to see my kids live out the values I've shared in this book. I've watched them grow strong and confident, and they are willing to live their lives, to take risks, and to help others. Those values were nurtured in me by my father and mother, and I'm proud to have been able to pass them on to the next generation.

I hope you do the same. I want to see you succeed, to find ways to reach out and give back to the community, and to live in a way that can make a difference. As you work on your personal and professional growth, look for ways to build your emotional intelligence. Know what you're worth and what you bring to the table. Manage what comes your way with a steady approach, just as my father did, despite living in a world of turmoil for decades.

After reading this book, I hope you'll reach out and get in touch. You can find me on LinkedIn. I'm always open to talking about crisis management, risk assessment, leadership, survival skills, and compliance. We can work together to contribute in a way that goes beyond our own selves. Together, we can share, grow, and make a difference for this generation of leaders—and the next.

ACKNOWLEDGMENTS

I want to thank all my family and friends who share my values and are part of my inner circle (you know who you are), for their continual commitment and support of me and what I stand for. I am forever grateful to my children, who teach me every day and who inspire me to be better. They've shown me a type of love and commitment that I didn't know existed. I am thankful to my husband Clinton who has been a solid, very present, and committed partner and father. I want to acknowledge my mother and my father, who were instrumental in establishing the values that I carry in my life, and my sister Valeria, for both her brilliant mind and ongoing companionship. I am thankful for the high-performing teams I have helped create and have been a part of—I would be willing to be kidnapped with you, and I am confident you would make the right decisions in critical moments. A special thanks to my longtime friendships including Cris, Dolo, Vicky S., Vero E., and las Margaritas from SMS.

I wanted to extend my sincere appreciation to those who helped develop this book, including Liz Archibald, Tati Akers, Dan Banks, Lucia Carrero-Rivera, Brenda Crabtree, Alicia Goodman, Donna Kinsey, Hans Peter Hasler, Randy Bagwell, Hanna Malak, and Andrew Oxtoby. Thank you to the team at Advantage/Forbes who guided every step of the process from the idea phase to publication. I want to acknowledge Rachel Hartman for her assistance in crafting and presenting the key messages in this book and adding magic to my words. Finally, thank you to my readers, for you are preparing yourselves to be better leaders for today and tomorrow—and can use the lessons in this book to positively impact the world around you. Ultimately, if I have helped one person to find their inner voice and their inner warrior, I have met my objectives.

ABOUT THE AUTHOR

As a seasoned C-level executive, Fabiana Lacerca-Allen has led global teams in the development and management of comprehensive compliance strategies and initiatives at Fortune 100 pharmaceutical and biotech companies. Lacerca-Allen is recognized for her ability to build compliance-based cultures and provide legal guidance to international leaders and boards. She is regularly sought out for crisis and risk management advice, and she influences leading companies on critical matters including product approval, commercialization, FDA and OIG compliance, mergers and acquisitions, joint ventures, and corporate governance.

Throughout her career, Lacerca-Allen has taken the lead to negotiate, implement, and carry out corporate integrity agreements, deferred prosecution agreements, and consent decrees. As a frequent keynote speaker and panelist, Lacerca-Allen regularly shares insights on compliance and crisis management with audiences of leaders and up-and-coming leaders. She is often asked to carry out security training and offers mentoring and advice to many professionals. Lacerca-Allen is also a trusted advisor and board member and has served in leadership positions at the American Red Cross, Shield Therapeutics, and Arthrocare, among others. Originally from Argentina and now residing in the US, Lacerca-Allen has traveled the world and prioritizes spending time with her family, including her husband and three children. Every day, she is driven to live out her values and make a difference in the world around her.

www.ingramcontent.com/pod-product-compliance
Lightning Source LLC
Chambersburg PA
CBHW020455100426
42813CB00031B/3373/J